JACQUELINE WILSON
The Homeschool Super Freak

It's HomEschooling, Not Solitary ConfinEmEnt

Busting the Myths, Misconceptions, and Misinformation About Homeschooling

It's Homeschooling, Not Solitary Confinement

Busting the Myths, Misconceptions, and Misinformation About Homeschooling

By

Jacqueline K. Wilson
The Homeschool Super Freak

Copyright ©2017 by Jacqueline K. Wilson and HomeschoolSuperFreak.com

All rights reserved.

No part of this publication may be reproduced, distributed, or transmitted in any form or by any means, including photocopying, recording, or other electronic or mechanical methods, without the prior written permission of the publisher, except in the case of brief quotations embodied in critical reviews and certain other noncommercial uses permitted by copyright law.

www.HomeschoolSuperFreak.com

Please contact info@MyPointMedia.com with questions.

First Printing July 2017

Published by MyPointMedia.com

INDIANAPOLIS, INDIANA

It's Homeschooling!
A companion journal to this book.

Learn more at
HomeschoolSuperFreak.com/Journal

PRAISE FROM HOMESCHOOLERS FOR *IT'S HOMESCHOOLING, NOT SOLITARY CONFINEMENT!*

"This book cleared up a lot of misconceptions and I can't wait to get it for my in-laws."
-Misty Fleener, homeschooling 1 year

"Wish I had this book 9 years ago when we started out on this journey - so much wisdom."
-Robin Blackburn, 8 years homeschooling two

"What a treasure trove of insight! I would highly recommend this book to anybody considering homeschooling!"
-Krystal Louder, homeschooling 7 years

"Amazed at the amount of information given in such an easy read! Don't skip the 'homework,' you'll end up with a journal of exactly what you want out of homeschooling and how to get it!"
-Becca Zurfley, homeschooling 2 years

"This was so helpful to me as someone just beginning our family's homeschooling journey! I loved the 'homework.' It really helped answer a lot of questions I had been musing over, and it inspired me to revisit topics I thought we'd settled. I can't wait for my husband to read it!"
-Mary S., beginning homeschooler

"An informative read for an aspiring homeschooler, in an easy-to-read format. I would definitely recommend this to anyone considering homeschooling. The opportunities for reflection at the end of each chapter are a great refresher for experienced homeschoolers, too!"
-Danielle Hayes, homeschooling 5 years

For all the unsocialized homeschoolers,
this one is for you.

The information referenced in this book relates specifically to homeschooling laws and requirements in the United States. If you live in another country, please check with your country's homeschooling laws. However, the general information about myths, misconceptions, and misinformation is still relevant.

The material provided in this book is informational only and not intended to be legal advice for homeschoolers and homeschooling. Please consult the homeschooling laws specific to your state and seek legal counsel and guidance if necessary.

So, you're thinking about homeschooling? Congratulations! You are exploring an exciting learning experience for your child and your entire family.

Or, maybe you're already homeschooling but you're worn down from all the negative comments, judgments, or the fact that you have to constantly explain your situation to friends, family members, and sometimes even complete strangers? I totally get it! Luckily, you've come to the right place for information, retorts, and support.

Whether you're a newbie homeschooler looking for answers to your questions, a seasoned homeschooler who is exhausted from all from all the misinformation, or even just curious about homeschooling, this book is for you.

Also, I know you're busy! That's why I've created a book with bite-sized bits of information so that you can take in one or two "snacks" at a time and not feel too overwhelmed with information. You can even skip around!

TABLE OF CONTENTS

Why This Book? 1

About The Author, Jacqueline Wilson 3

Getting Started 9

Myth #1: "Everyone should homeschool." 13

Myth #2: "I think you can go to jail for that." 19

Myth #3: "Your child will never be socialized!" 25

Myth #4: "Only religious or weirdo freaks homeschool." .35

Myth #5: "You need a college degree or teaching experience to homeschool." 39

Myth #6: "I can't homeschool because I have no idea where to start." 43

Myth #7: "I'm not sure if I want to homeschool all the way through high school, so I don't think I should start." 53

Myth #8: "Homeschooling is just regular school, but at home in your pajamas." 55

Myth #9: "You have to keep your kids inside during school hours or child protective services will visit." 59

Myth #10: "It's too expensive to homeschool." 63

Myth #11: "Homeschool kids can't play sports." 67

Myth #12: "You cannot work or contribute financially to your family if you homeschool." 72

(Or: "I don't have time for homeschooling.") 71

Myth #13: "Kids need the structure of a traditional school to be successful." 75

Myth #14: "Homeschool kids have a hard time getting accepted into college." 81

Myth #15: "It's important for kids to experience real life and they just can't get that from homeschooling." 85

Myth #16: "You will never know if your kids have learned anything." 91

Myth #17: "I don't have the patience to homeschool." 99

Myth #18: "Homeschoolers hate when you ask them questions." 105

Myth #19: "Something terrible must have happened to you in school for you to choose homeschooling." 109

Myth #20: "I don't have room in my house for a classroom so I can't homeschool." 113

Myth #21: "You'll never be able to have a sick day." 117

Myth #22: "Homeschool kids rely too much on their parents, so they'll never be independent." 121

Myth #23: "Homeschooling is too boring for kids." 125

Myth #24: "Your kids will never be able to distinguish between your parent role and your teacher role." 129

Myth #25: "You have to listen to what the public school system tells you, so you're better off just sending your kids to regular school." 135

Myth #26: "Your kids will never go to prom." 139

Myth #27: "Go ahead, homeschool your kid, but you won't have any support." 143

Myth #28: "You can't homeschool because your child has special needs / is struggling / learns differently." 147

Myth #29: "Your kid will miss out on *so much* not going to regular school." 151

Myth #30: "Homeschooling just isn't a 'proper education.'" 153

Other Silly Things Homeschoolers Hear 155

References 161

"Knowledge that is acquired under compulsion obtains no hold on the mind."
-Plato

"Expect to observe a notable surge in the number of children being homeschooled in the next 5 to 10 years."

- Dr. Brian Ray, NHERI.org, 2012

Why This Book?

I started writing this book in 2016 after talking to a group of homeschool moms. At the time, we were discussing all the same questions that we hear over and over again from our in-laws, our friends, our family, and even strangers when we're out in public during "school hours." I came home that day and started writing a list of the most asked questions that homeschoolers hear. Over time, I added more and more to the list and I was astonished at all the myths and misinformation out there about homeschooling—the ridiculousness of some of the questions were humorous, while some of the more judgmental myths were painful to hear. Some of the misinformation, however, stemmed from the fact that no one had told the person differently or opened interesting discussions between people of differing learning styles or methods.

It was during that time that I also realized these myths, misconceptions, and misinformation could deter would-be homeschoolers from choosing this educational track for their family. And, as someone who is trained in research, I want people to have a wide spectrum of information so that they can make the best decisions.

For these reasons, I knew I wanted to put a book out there in order to help clear the air about homeschooling—not just for the people who were making these judgments and spreading false information, but for people who really wanted to learn about homeschooling. You know, the truth versus misinformation. I also wanted to give some information and rebuttals for homeschoolers when they get asked these common questions. This is my attempt to provide some answers to some of the questions that people have and to correct some of the more common myths, misconceptions, and misinformation.

If you are exploring homeschooling or are new to homeschooling, you may have some of the questions covered in this book. And that's OK! We all did at some point. This book has your answers!

About The Author, Jacqueline Wilson

I'm Jacqueline Wilson, The Homeschool Super Freak.

The name *Homeschool Super Freak* came from an inside joke with other homeschoolers. There is a perception in society that homeschoolers are "freaks." (Maybe we are?) So, our group would jokingly (and lovingly) refer to ourselves as "homeschool freaks." Laughing, one day I blurted out, "I'm not a homeschool freak, I'm a homeschool SUPER freak." And . . . a concept was born.

I've been homeschooling for over five years now but have been in the education field in some capacity for 16 years. I write and edit academically—books, study guides, and college courses—and have probably written and edited over 50 books or guides for college courses. (I've lost count at this point.)

I hold a Bachelor of Science, a specialized healthcare certification, and a partial Master's Degree in Distance Education (I should probably finish it, but I'm too busy, you know . . . homeschooling my kid). I am also the founder and executive director of a nonprofit organization.

In addition to homeschooling, some of the things I do

include: wife, mother, educator, soapbox stander, academic writer, published author, speaker, consultant, accidental pit bull advocate, and discriminating sock monkey enthusiast.

I have a small collection of rescued pets in my home. One more and I get a free set of steak knives!

(Don't judge me.)

Our Homeschooling Story

I first started thinking about homeschooling my daughter when she was almost three years old. She went to a Montessori preschool and loved it; she thrived there. However, I couldn't help but feel that there was something more that could be happening with her education. There was a whole world of freedom and exposure to learning out there. And, I was worried about the life skills that she wasn't being exposed to by sitting at a desk in a classroom for hours each day. She had, *maybe,* thirty minutes of outdoor play in a small yard sandwiched between a brick building and a concrete parking structure. It just wasn't working for me. Something just didn't *feel* right about educating my child this way. (You may be nodding your head in agreement right now!)

I'll never forget when I finally worked up enough courage to discuss homeschooling with my husband. It did seem kind of *out there*, even in my head, so how was my husband going to react?

"So," I said to my husband over dinner one night. "I think I'm going to homeschool Ella when she gets to kindergarten age."

He stared at me for a few minutes like I had lost my mind.

"No," he replied, shaking his head vehemently.

"What do you mean, 'no?'" I asked.

"Just . . . no," he shrugged. "Why would you ever want to do that when she can just . . . *go to school*? It's weird."

It's weird.

And that was my first glimpse into the judgments, questions, myths, misconceptions, and more that I would experience as a homeschooling parent. To be honest, I had no idea what I was getting myself into. I didn't know that almost everyone in my life would have input or judgments about homeschooling. Some were innocent questions by people who were genuinely curious ("What curriculum will you use?" or "What made you want to homeschool?") and others had a more judgmental bite ("You'll never get her caught up when she has to go to a real school because this doesn't work.") And, some people were downright hateful about it. ("She'll become a shy, backwards freak.")

Ouch.

It wasn't until 2011 when we had an interstate move that I got serious about the subject of homeschooling. By then, my husband was open to the idea but still very, very skeptical. (I had worn him down.) My daughter went to a

Montessori preschool in our new state while I set out to learn everything I could about homeschooling over the next six months. I studied state laws. I spent hours and hours reviewing curricula online until my eyes crossed. I read homeschooling blogs and books. I asked newbie questions about testing and playgroups and reporting requirements. I cried. I gnashed teeth. I doubted myself. I got excited. And then, in 2012, I started homeschooling my daughter at the age of four.

During my research, I had put together a binder, color coded by section and subject, and listed out a *very* detailed schedule that we would follow during our homeschooling day. I had done my research, so this had to work, right? I had a *color-coded binder*, what could go wrong?

By noon on the first day, I hid in the kitchen pantry and cried (the ugly snotty kind). For real. Everything I had studied and planned and organized–that huge, color-coded binder–fell apart by 12 o'clock on that first day. But, I learned one valuable lesson: **I planned too much**. I didn't realize one of the best things about homeschooling is **just allowing learning to flow**. I was homeschooling like a traditional school. We were on a tight schedule by precise topics. And, that's not really what homeschooling is about . . . *at all*. (But, more on that later.)

Five years later, I still fail. But, I succeed far more.

And I still get the homeschool questions and the judgments. I have to deal with many myths, misconceptions, and as much misinformation about homeschooling now as I did when I first started.

What I've done in this book is address some of that misinformation so it will help you better understand the truth about homeschooling. This book will equip you with information that will help you to make the best decision about educating your own children and maybe even give you some verbal ammunition for defending your choice.

If you're here just because you're curious about homeschooling, I applaud you for that, too!

Getting Started

Before you start, I recommend that you grab a notebook and pen and have them ready as you read through the book and work on some of the "homework" assignments that I put in here for you. That's right! I put in some takeaways just to help you understand homeschooling a little better. This will help you collect notes, thoughts, and resources in one place so you can refer back to them later.

I also have a companion *It's Just Homeschooling! Planner & Journal* that is perfect for keeping track of the things you learn from this book and helping you plan for homeschooling. It corresponds to the homework sections provided in this book and includes the questions and prompts so you don't need to write them out again. Not only will it help you plan your homeschooling time, but it also gives you plenty of journaling and note-taking space!

You can find more information on the *It's Homeschooling! Planner & Journal* on the website at:

HomeschoolSuperFreak.com/Journal

Why Use a Journal?

Paper is to write things down that we need to remember. Our brains are used to think.

—Albert Einstein

Did you know that writing things down increases your chance of remembering them? That's why I think it's important, especially if you're new to homeschooling or just researching the option, to not just read through the book, but to also spend time documenting the takeaways as well as journaling and planning for a successful homeschooling experience.

In this book, I have also listed references for each chapter at the end of the book. If you want to do a little more research on that topic, you have the references handy and don't have to search the internet for further information.

A Quick Note About Social Media

Lastly, a bit of advice: connect with other homeschoolers, both in your area and online! Social media sites like Facebook, Instagram, Twitter, and others are all fantastic ways to stay connected in the homeschool community. Not only will you meet new friends that help create an online support system, you will also gather ideas and information on homeschooling and stay current on national and state homeschool laws, regulations, and updates.

Be sure to create a network of other homeschoolers that you can bounce ideas off of and who will pick you up on the days that you've fallen or feel defeated. Use the online world to supplement your in-person homeschool support system.

New To Social Media? Reluctant To Join? Read This!

If you're not on social media yet, I encourage you to join because you are missing out on the active online homeschool communities! Facebook, Twitter, Instagram, and Snapchat are online social media platforms that allow to you to connect with others and (the best part) they are free to join!

I suggest starting with Facebook because there are tons of homeschooling websites, blogs, and pages geared toward the topic of homeschooling. There may even be homeschool meet up groups local to you, so you can connect online and then meet up with a group in person!

If you haven't joined Facebook (or other social media platforms) because you don't want to be surrounded by "drama," I get it. However, there are ways to get around it. I've been on social media for YEARS and I've pretty much created a drama-free bubble where I see only the things I want to see. And you can do that, too!

Join us on Facebook at:

Facebook.com/HomeschoolSuperFreak

It's an amazing group of homeschoolers at all stages and levels who foster interesting, intelligent, and respectful discussion. Plus, there are lots of things over there to make you laugh . . . which we all need a little more of, right? We would love to have you as part of the conversation! And, we promise to pick you up when you need it!

Let's get started!

Myth #1: "Everyone should homeschool."

There are some homeschooling parents who believe, without question, that people should homeschool. They are die-hard homeschool families and think homeschooling is the best educational system for children. The end. I can respect the passion these families have because homeschooling is an amazing learning opportunity for kids and a great experience for families. However, many other homeschool families think that homeschooling is not for everyone.

I happen to fall into that group.

This may surprise you coming from someone who spends a great deal of time writing about homeschooling, but I don't happen to think homeschooling is for everyone. I don't want people to tell me how I should educate my daughter, so I sure don't want to tell others the best educational route for their own children. It does not mean that everyone cannot homeschool or that people who choose homeschooling are an elite group of people who are better than those who do not choose homeschooling. Instead, it just means that you should be able to choose the way that you want your child educated.

Homeschooling is a serious topic that should be given serious consideration and research. It's hard, it's time consuming, and it's exhausting. If you are not committed to it, then it will not work. (Motivated yet?) I often say that homeschooling is the hardest thing I have ever done. It's way harder than when I worked over 80 hours a week in the corporate world for someone else. However, it's much more rewarding and it's a fulfilling kind of exhaustion—that accomplished tiredness you feel at the end of a productive day, you know?

Recently, we moved to a different neighborhood. One of the things that we did when we moved is downsize. The house we had before was too big and I felt like I was chasing the house. I was never caught up with housework and always stressed. When you are homeschooling you don't need additional things to stress about during your day. So, as part of the moving and downsizing process, we got rid of a lot of stuff—like three full moving trailers full of donations! (Yes, it was embarrassing to type that.)

Once we moved into the new house, I worked like a maniac to get things in their place downstairs. It wasn't that I had a deadline to meet for that area, it was just that the more tired I felt the more I wanted things to be in their place. I was exhausted, beyond tired really, but I wouldn't stop until our first floor was unpacked and everything was in place. Once things were clean and put away in the proper place, I felt like I could breathe again. I was exhausted, but it was a good tired filled with accomplishment. You know that feeling? That's exactly how homeschool exhaustion feels. You're tired, but when you see your child grasping a concept or you see the light in your child's eyes when they experience something new, it makes the exhaustion worth it.

So no, I don't think homeschooling is for everyone, but that doesn't mean you can't do it. In fact, I *know* you can. But, you need to be clear about the responsibilities, requirements, and time commitments. It's no joke and is not to be taken lightly.

Related Myth: "Homeschooling families are against traditional schools."

In one education study, a large portion of homeschool parents–91 percent of those parents surveyed–listed "a concern about the environment of other schools" as their reason for homeschooling. It's true that many homeschool families are concerned about public schools today, but that doesn't make us against traditional schools. It just means that something about traditional schooling is not working for *our children*. Just like we want the ability to choose the best schooling option for our children, many homeschool parents want other parents to be able to choose the option that works best for their family. In many cases, that is obviously traditional public school.

If you find a homeschooler who is willing to have an honest and respectful discussion, most of us will not preach about removing children from public schools and placing them into alternative learning. However, many homeschooling parents, as well as many public school educators and other parents, do believe that the current educational system is broken. That doesn't necessarily make homeschooling families against traditional school.

Homeschool Homework 1

Review the reasons you're homeschooling or considering homeschooling.

1. Divide a sheet of paper into two columns. On one side list "Homeschooling Pros" and on the other side list "Homeschooling Cons." (You can also use the corresponding section in the *It's Homeschooling!* companion journal.)

2. Set a timer for five minutes and come up with reasons for the pros and cons list. Don't give it too much thought! Just write down the first things that come to mind. Continue until the timer goes off.

3. Review your lists. Are there more pros or more cons? Are some of them just myths about homeschooling? (If you're

not sure, keep reading!)

JACQUELINE WILSON

Myth #2: "I think you can go to jail for that."

No, you're not going to jail for legitimately homeschooling your child in the United States (at least not at the time this book was published). However, this myth has some basis in truth if you were homeschooling not so long ago in the United States. In some states, homeschooling was still illegal as recently as 1993. (Weird, right?) In homeschooling years, that's not very long ago. To fully understand homeschooling legalities, let's first take a brief look into the history of homeschooling.

Homeschooling was actually the norm in early America, going as far back as colonial times when people came over on the Mayflower. Then, it was standard to school your children at home while completing all the other homesteading chores. It wasn't until 1837 when Massachusetts opened its first public school that the move toward compulsory education started.

According to the Georgia Home Education Association (GHEA), the first public school created the "first statewide school system in which schools were centralized, state controlled, and financed by property taxes" and "was the beginning of state-controlled secular education and the first significant loss of freedom for individuals and families in Massachusetts and, consequently, the entire country." By 1918, all states enacted compulsory education, requiring children to attend school, and making homeschooling a crime in all states.

Jump forward a few decades to the liberating 1960s and 70s when homeschooling started to gain a widespread interest again. However, at that point removing children from public schools to homeschool was illegal. According to the Home School Legal Defense Association (HSLDA), school officials called the process of removing a child from a public school to a home school "criminal truancy."

During this time, when parents removed children to homeschool, the traditional schools recorded the amount of time that children were out of the school as unexcused absences instead of a withdrawal from the school. This forced parents who wanted to homeschool to take an illegal underground approach. Some parents started the homeschool process before children were ever enrolled in the traditional school system so that no public school record of the kids existed. Some families even went as far as to move to a new community where their children were never enrolled in that local school system. Unbelievably, some parents were still fined or even served jail time for simply wanting to teach their children at home.

Right before this time, Nevada and Utah had started

to allow homeschooling. Nevada passed homeschooling legislation in 1956, followed closely by Utah in 1957. It wasn't until 24 years later in the 1980s, that other states followed. By 1989, Michigan, North Dakota, and Iowa were the only three states that still considered homeschooling illegal. By 1993, all 50 states had enacted legislation to make homeschooling legal.

Today, homeschooling legal requirements vary based on the state where you live. Homeschooling laws differ about as much as the reasons for homeschooling! For example, Indiana (the state where I live) has some of the most relaxed homeschooling laws. I am not required to report anything to the school system unless I am transferring my child out of public school. Then, a letter of intent is needed. I do not have to use specific curricula or have my child tested. I am required to "provide equivalent education" to public school and also document attendance that shows I have completed at least 180 days of school study in case I am required to provide it to child protective services, to schools, or for some other legal reason.

On the other end of the spectrum, there are some states that have very stringent homeschool reporting guidelines. These states might including requirements like notifying schools of your intent to homeschool, reporting achievement scores, using only a state-approved tutor as the homeschooling teacher, using only state-approved curricula, or being subjected to site visits by state officials. The homeschooling guidelines in Massachusetts, the state that first started compulsory education, remain quite rigorous. There, homeschooling is equated to "private schooling" and a homeschool program must be approved by the state. Also in that state, school officials can ask for the parent's qualification as a teacher, review the subjects to be studied, ask for the length of the homeschool year and hours of instructional time, and require standardized testing, periodic progress reports, or any other evaluation method.

As you can see, homeschooling laws can be quite diverse. Although homeschooling is not illegal, it is important to understand the laws that govern homeschooling for your state, or even a state where you and your family are going to be temporarily located.

Homeschool Homework 2

Stop now and check the homeschooling laws in your state. Use the links below to get started.

Visit:

Home School Legal Defense Association (HSLDA) at

https://www.hslda.org/laws/

Education and Homeschooling State Laws at

http://education.findlaw.com/education-options/education-and-homeschooling-state-laws.html

You can also search the internet for "homeschooling laws [your state]" for further information.

Be sure to note any laws applicable to your state in your journal or notebook.

Homeschool Extra

Want to read more about homeschooling history? Check this out:

The Politics of Survival: Home Schoolers and the Law at

https://www.hslda.org/docs/nche/000010/PoliticsOfSurvival.asp

Remember, the laws referenced in this book relate specifically to homeschooling laws in the United States. If you live in another country, please check with your country's homeschooling laws.

JACQUELINE WILSON

Myth #3: "Your child will never be socialized!"

The title of this book, *It's Homeschooling, Not Solitary Confinement,* came from a meme I made on our Homeschool Super Freak Facebook page. Robin (from Batman and Robin) is asking the big, green Hulk, "But if you homeschool how will your kids get socialization?" And the Hulk, fists clenched, is barking back, "It's homeschooling, not solitary confinement!"

If you've been homeschooling for some time, you're probably chuckling a little at this right now. If you're just now considering homeschooling, you'll get our collective eye roll soon enough because that panicked look from people and the question *"How will you ever socialize your child?"* is one of the most frequent questions that we get from those who don't understand homeschooling. (*"It's homeschooling, not solitary confinement!"* is one of my favorite and frequent retorts.)

When people make this comment, it's difficult to know if they really mean *socialized* or *socialization*. According to Dictionary.com, **socialized** means "to associate or mingle sociably with others," while **socialization** means "a continuing process whereby an individual acquires a personal identity and learns the norms, values, behavior, and social skills appropriate to his or her social position." I'm guessing that people really mean *socialization*, but both are relevant to the discussion of homeschooling. What I think people really mean is some form of "How will your child ever learn to interact with others?"

This may be one of your own concerns if you're just now researching the homeschooling option. To be honest, it was a big concern for me before I truly understood the homeschooling process. *How will I make sure that my social butterfly is being fulfilled and that she fits into society?* It weighed on my mind until I came to a full understanding that **I control what I do in homeschooling and how my child learns, including when to be with other kids in group learning situations like play dates or classes outside of the home.** You have that full control, too. If you're like most homeschooling families, your kids will have a great deal of group learning opportunities outside of the home.

Related Myth: "Homeschool kids aren't exposed to diversity."

For those who don't understand the homeschool process, there seems to be a general misconception that homeschooled kids are reclusive and never get the opportunity to interact with others, both in their peer group and with those of different ages and backgrounds. Some may even think that homeschool kids will never be able to develop the social skills that will carry them through life. In fact, it's just the opposite.

The National Home Education Resource Institute (NHERI), an organization that collects and publishes information on homeschooling, reports that homeschooled kids "participate in approximately five different social activities outside the home on a regular basis." Furthermore, researcher Dr. Linda Montgomery found that "78 percent of high school home learners were employed with paying jobs, while a majority engaged in volunteering and community service." These are all ways that homeschooled kids are exposed to a diverse group of individuals, age ranges, and belief systems, just like in real life.

Let's back up for a second and repeat, *you control what you do in homeschooling*. It seems like common sense, but this actually took a little while to sink in for me. I was so rooted in traditional school methods that I was missing the most important part of homeschooling: **total control**! You can get your children as involved as you want (or as they want) in outside activities that help them be social with a diverse group. For us, in addition to our at-home learning, my daughter attends swimming, Spanish class, American Heritage Girls (which is a group like Girl Scouts), music, cooking classes, and others, all outside of the home. Additionally, we participate in periodic classes or events offered through local parks, nature centers, libraries, and museums. That doesn't even count the meet ups and play dates we do with friends, both homeschooled and traditionally schooled.

I'll never forget a time right after I started homeschooling when we went to an event with mechanical dinosaurs. (My kid was obsessed with dinosaurs!) At this event, you learned about dinosaur food preferences and how they lived. There were also mechanical dinosaur rides. As my daughter rode one of the dinosaurs, I noticed that a ride attendant was having a long conversation with her. At the end of the ride, the worker brought her back over and said, "Your daughter is so outgoing for a homeschooled kid!" (Something we've heard a lot over the years of homeschooling.)

The truth is this: your kid's personality is your kid's personality, no matter if he or she is homeschooled or goes to a public school or a private school. There are introverted homeschooled kids and there are outgoing and boisterous homeschooled kids, just like in traditional schools.

Homeschooling your kids and getting them involved in different activities with a diverse group of kids outside the home is a great way to encourage socialization. It's also way more realistic to their future interactions as opposed to just sitting in a classroom all day with kids their own age, right?

Supplementing Your Homeschooling

We are blessed to live in an area that has ample opportunities for classes outside of the home. The local library now offers a full schedule of different homeschool classes, from writing and math to art and foreign languages. We also have several opportunities to join nature or farm schools that teach kids about wilderness, farm life, and being outside.

My daughter is a farmer at heart (and we are *so* not). If my daughter attended a traditional school, she would not have the opportunity to learn in an environment that she loves as much as wilderness and farming. Instead, we would have to wait for a summer camp that would fulfill her interests for a few days or one week out of an entire year. Now, we can enroll her in these wilderness and farm programs that allow her to cultivate her interests on a regular basis.

You will probably have the same kind of opportunities in your area—no matter where you live (even if you have to drive to find them)! Maybe your child isn't interested in farming, but maybe she is interested in cooking, or art, or architecture, or robotics. As a homeschooling parent, it's your responsibility to match at-home learning and outside learning to your child's interests and your child's learning style. As a homeschooling parent, I have the freedom to supplement her learning as I see fit and so do you. **You have that freedom! Don't forget to use it!**

Let's take a closer look at a couple of examples of the supplemental education available to homeschoolers and where to find it. These are great ways to get your kids out and interacting with other homeschooled children. (You know, that whole socialization thing again.)

Co-ops

If you live in an area where homeschooling is popular, you probably have something called co-ops readily available to you. In some cases, you may have to drive to find a co-op (or even start one!). Either way, it is another way to supplement your homeschooling with some outside-the-home learning with groups of children.

Co-op is short for *cooperative*. With a homeschooling co-op, homeschoolers come together to offer different learning opportunities. In academic co-ops, there may be a designated educator who sets a specific curriculum. In other academic co-ops, parental involvement is the key and parents may be asked to lead an educational session. There are some co-ops that stick to a strict classical curriculum and there are others that are more relaxed in their learning styles. There are also social co-ops that are just for meeting up, playing, and organizing field trips. If you decide to supplement your at-home learning by joining a co-op, you can determine what style of co-op works best for your family.

Homeschool Classes

The National Center for Education Statistics (NCES), part of the U.S. Department of Education, collects and publishes information on education in America. The organization projects that homeschooling has grown from 850,000 children in 1990 to 1.5 million children in 2007. Today, we see statistics as high as 1.7 million homeschooling children in the United States.

As the homeschooling movement continues to grow and gain momentum across the country, many businesses are now offering homeschool programs. Nature centers, zoos, museums, libraries, and more are jumping on the homeschooling train and offering free or low-cost classes to homeschoolers. Some of these may be one-time class sessions and others may be ongoing homeschool classes where your child can develop relationships with other homeschoolers.

As you can see, there are plenty of opportunities to get your child out and interacting with other kids—plenty of opportunities to be "social."

Related Myth: "Homeschooled kids are less confident than other kids."

Another myth that fits perfectly within this discussion is about the confidence of a homeschooled child. There is a public perception that homeschooled children are less confident (we also hear: *shy, awkward, backward, withdrawn,* and plenty more that aren't as nice as those descriptions). Here's the truth: if a child is shy, he or she is going to be shy no matter how or where they attend school. And, as we discussed earlier, the same is true if a student is outgoing and boisterous. He or she is going to be that way no matter what.

We happen to spend a great deal of time outside the home in mixed groups of kids—some of my daughter's outside classes are only homeschoolers, some are a mix of homeschool and traditional school kids, and in some classes, my daughter is the only homeschooled child. In one of those classes a mom of a traditionally schooled child said to me, "I always notice how polite and respectful your daughter is. She carries herself so well." I don't think this is just a direct result of homeschooling. Instead, I happen to think that it has more to do with our expectations at home . . . which comes from parenting and not necessarily homeschooling.

In this same class, another child called my daughter a degrading name and made fun of her for something. My daughter had no idea that it was a bad thing. In this case, I do happen to think that my daughter's reaction *is* a result of homeschooling because my daughter is not around a group of kids who regularly peer pressure her like what may happen in traditional school. She was very matter of fact when she recounted the story to me but, internally, I was seething. I actually had to explain to her the meaning of the word and encourage her to tell the other little girl not to refer to her that way.

In many cases, you will find that homeschooled kids are confident in who they are—even if they are shy, outgoing, or somewhere in between. I believe that's because most homeschooled children are in an environment where they are allowed to fail without societal or peer repercussions. They are given the love, support, and room needed to fail and be supported in those failures without being in a peer group who will make fun of them for failing. Many homeschooled kids are allowed to just be who they are and grow confident in that, which also makes them comfortable with others who are different from them.

Homeschool Homework 3

Research extracurricular programs, homeschool programs, and co-ops in your area.

(You don't have to make any commitments. Remember, we're just in the researching stage right now!)

1. Talk to your child and get to know what they're really interested in learning. (You might be surprised because it could be completely different than what you think!) Write down some of your child's interests in your notebook or journal. Then, search the internet for those programs in your area. Review some of the options that come up. Note the days, times, and costs of the programs. This will help give you an idea of how you will plan your at-home learning and your out-of-home learning. Plus, this pre-planning will help you budget.

2. Now, search the Internet for homeschool programs at local businesses in your area (or your state). Be sure to search zoos, museums, parks, libraries, and nature centers. Sometimes you can find them online by searching the business websites or Facebook pages, or by using a search engine to search "homeschool day camps." Add the information to your homeschooling research notes.

3. Lastly, search the internet for homeschooling co-ops in your city. If none show up for your city, try searching your state instead. Also, search for homeschooling co-op Facebook groups for your area. If you're comfortable, request to join the group and read through some of the postings.

Myth #4: "Only religious or weirdo freaks homeschool."

Whoa. Whoa. Whoa. Simmer down, there.

People who don't know much about homeschooling sometimes assume that homeschoolers are made up of just a few unusual families here and there who are homeschooling for religious reasons. Some parts of society have this image that homeschoolers make up a very small percentage of people who look like they stepped out of *Little House on the Prairie* and isolate their families like "freaks." (And, of course, you should know by now that we aren't freaks . . . we're homeschool *super* freaks!)

However, these people may be surprised to learn that there are an estimated 1.7 million homeschoolers—or about 3.4 percent of the school-age population—in the United States. That's certainly not an insignificant number! (And, if we're all freaks, then there are *a lot* of freaks roaming around!)

Out of the homeschooling parents who answered The National Household Education Surveys (NHES) program survey of 2012—which is the latest published aggregate on homeschool data—64 percent reported "a desire to provide religious instruction" as their reason for homeschooling. However, it was not the top reason parents listed for homeschooling. A whopping 91 percent listed "a concern about the environment of other schools" as their reason for homeschooling. Although we cannot be sure the exact reasoning behind these concerns (for example, parents may be concerned about the lack of religious instructions for this category), it is clear that parents are no longer electing to homeschool solely based on religious reasons.

There have historically been two polarizing groups of homeschooling families—Christian homeschooling families, who homeschool for religious reasons, and progressive homeschooling families, who prefer non-traditional educational methods that have nothing to do with religion. However, there seems to be much more fluidity in the homeschooling movement today, with homeschool families falling somewhere in the middle. There are still many homeschool families who educate at home for Bible-based learning. There are also homeschool parents who teach religious studies during homeschool, but that may not be their biggest motivation for homeschooling. Other homeschooling parents do not consider themselves religious and do not homeschool for this reason nor incorporate this topic into their learning.

The point is this: no matter your belief system or reasons for homeschooling, there's a place for you. We have homeschooling friends of all different backgrounds and affiliations. There is a great deal of diversity in homeschooling today! You can learn a lot from each other if you open yourself to it.

Homeschool Homework 4

Spend some time thinking about why you want to homeschool. Set a timer for five minutes and brainstorm the reasons–be sure to document them in your companion journal or notebook. These reasons will be a good reminder as you travel through your homeschooling journey. It will also be interesting to see how your reasons grow and change over your time homeschooling.

JACQUELINE WILSON

Myth #5: "You need a college degree or teaching experience to homeschool."

I'm going to let you in on a little secret that may blow your mind: as soon as our kids are born, they start learning! As parents, we start teaching our kids at first contact with them. (Mind. Blown. I know!) You've already been teaching your child even if you aren't a homeschooling parent. However, for some reason, as soon as we put a title on it ("homeschooling parent"), we get nervous and start thinking we're not good enough (not smart enough, not educated enough, *whatever*) to lead our kids in learning. When, in reality, that's what we're doing every day anyway, no matter where a child goes to school.

And, guess what else? You *can* homeschool and you *do not* need to be a former teacher or have a formal college education to do so. With that said, there are some states that do require homeschooling parents to have some level of education in order to homeschool. For those states, the requirement is most often a high school diploma or GED. Currently, those states are: Georgia, New Mexico, North Carolina, North Dakota, Ohio, Pennsylvania, South Carolina, Tennessee, Virginia, Washington, and West Virginia. If you live in one of these states, or will be homeschooling in one of these states, be sure to further research the parental background requirements needed in order to homeschool.

But, what if you aren't strong in a specific subject? (Read on . . .)

Related Myth: "You aren't strong enough/smart enough to teach all topics."

Another variation of this myth goes something like this: "You are terrible in math [or, insert another subject here], how are you going to teach that?" There is definitely a little truth to this; however, it's mainly because people misunderstand the homeschooling process (once again). I don't speak Spanish, but my daughter wanted to learn Spanish. So, we enrolled her in an outside Spanish class. She goes twice a week and loves it. Problem solved.

If there are subjects that you are uncomfortable teaching, there are plenty of courses, online classes, and curricula that will guide you through the homeschool learning process and help you with every topic you want to include in your homeschool studies–even the ones that you find difficult. There are options for every topic that you are not comfortable tackling on your own with your child. Yes, even math. (You're welcome.)

Homeschool Homework 5
Research parental homeschooling qualifications for

your state.

Search online for "homeschool parent qualifications [your state]" in order to better understand the parental homeschool requirements for your state. Note the requirements in your journal or notebook.

Homeschool Extra

Also check out *Parent Qualifications Quick Facts* at:

https://www.responsiblehomeschooling.org/policy-issues/current-policy/parent-qualifications/

JACQUELINE WILSON

Myth #6: "I can't homeschool because I have no idea where to start."

I have more great news! I know, it seems like I keep saying that, but it really *is* an exciting time to be homeschooling. There are almost endless resources for you and many of them are free! Whether you are a brand new homeschooler or a seasoned homeschooler who wants to try out something new, chances are someone has gone there before you and has written a book, developed a curriculum, created a blog, offered an online class, or started a meet up or an online social media group. There are also plenty of websites that offer free or low-cost lessons, worksheets, craft instructions, and more. You will rarely have to reinvent the wheel because it's probably already out there. So, you don't have to be intimidated to start homeschooling because so many have gone before you now. You just need to research what others have done and then pick a path that you want to take as a homeschooling family.

When I first started, I did not know any homeschooling families. I had not connected with any other homeschooling parents to create a support network. (Big mistake, by the way.) I didn't have anyone to tell me how to approach it, what to do first, and what can wait until later. Now I wish I had known more about homeschooling methods. **Understanding what method you want to use for homeschooling is a good starting place for a new homeschooler.**

Understanding Homeschool Methods and Styles

Methods, styles, and approaches are terms often used interchangeably to simply mean how you're going to approach homeschooling. Do you want your child's learning to include classical traits or Latin? Do you want your child to be able to choose what he or she wants to study each day? Are you someone who likes to pick and choose the best things from different programs and create your own lessons and curricula? Are you a laid-back person or do you like things to be completed in an orderly fashion? All of this (and more) will guide how you approach homeschooling. (By the way, it's OK if you don't know the answer to any of these questions yet!)

Let's take a quick look at some different homeschooling methods. These are just a few short examples, so I recommend that you do more extensive online research. This certainly is not a comprehensive or an all-inclusive list and is meant to provide examples only. (Methods can be an entire book on its own!)

Charlotte Mason Homeschoolers

The biggest goal of Charlotte Mason homeschooling is to focus on the child as a whole person and not just the mind. Charlotte Mason lists three specific points: *education as an atmosphere, education as a discipline, and education as a life.*

The Charlotte Mason method uses short lessons that allow kids to focus fully on their learning for short periods of time. This method also encourages good habits, focuses on having a child to think and expressive himself or herself clearly, and uses processes like dictation for spelling. The Charlotte Mason method is a big advocate of music, art, and nature studies, and encourages children to spend as much time outside as possible.

Eclectic Homeschoolers

Eclectic homeschooling is sometimes referred to as *relaxed homeschooling*. Eclectic homeschool families use a variety of methods and resources for homeschool learning. For example, an eclectic homeschooling parent may use a curriculum for one area, like history, but then use an unschooling approach for another subject area like art, where they allow the child to choose what they want to learn. Eclectic homeschooling allows you to pick and choose the best items from different curricula, styles, and methods and tailor them to best meet your family's needs.

Unschoolers

An unschooling approach is also called *child-lead learning* or *natural learning*. With unschooling, parents allow the child to take the lead in what they want to learn and how they want to learn it. It is based on a method made famous by homeschool proponent John Holt, an educator from Yale University who believes that children learn subject matter naturally. For example, instead of learning from textbooks and worksheets, an unschooling approach might incorporate a child's interest of cooking as a way of learning science and math naturally from recipes. Cooking is great way for children to learn basic addition and subtraction when determining how many cups or tablespoons are needed, as well as a way to learn about more advanced concepts like fractions. Additionally, cooking is a fun way to learn science principals like chemical reactions and also about liquids, gases, and solids. With an unschooling approach, it is believed that the child will learn those concepts naturally as they spend time experiencing things like cooking and reading recipes.

Classical Homeschoolers

The classical method of homeschooling, sometimes called the Socratic method, is divided into different tools of learning called *Trivium*. Trivium is broken into *reason, record, research, relate,* and *rhetoric*. Classical homeschoolers base their learning on the styles of classical thinkers like Aristotle, Thomas Jefferson, and C.S. Lewis. This method often includes Latin and classical literature.

Cross-Curriculum Homeschoolers

Cross-curriculum homeschoolers base their learning on unit topics. For example, cross-curriculum homeschoolers may take a topic their child is interested in, like sea turtles, and then build (or buy) a learning unit that includes all areas–math, science, language, etc.–around that topic.

As you can see just from these short examples, there are many different methods that you can choose for homeschooling. If your homeschooling is centered around Bible-based learning with a focus on respect and teaching the whole child (and not just the mind), then you may want to check out the Charlotte Mason Method. If you're interested in a classical education that focuses more on children's cognitive development, then you may be more interested in the classical or Socratic method of homeschooling. If you like a mix of learning styles, then the eclectic approach might be good for your family.

If you're reading through these learning styles and thinking, "I have no idea what style I am!" then don't worry! You don't have to adhere to any specific style . . . and you certainly don't have to determine your method right away. Realistically, you'll probably choose to teach from a variety of methods that meet your family's needs based on schedules, topics, learning styles, and available materials, especially in the beginning of your homeschooling journey.

And, here's some more good news: **You don't have to define any method at all.** You can just do what works for your family! We do a mix of eclectic, cross-curriculum, and unschooling right now. As my daughter gets older, we may gear our studies to a more classical approach, but for now this mix of methods is working for us.

Again, if you're new to homeschooling and you have absolutely no idea how you want your homeschooled child to learn, that's okay! When you're first starting, just learning about the different homeschooling methods can be completely overwhelming. Remember when I hid in the pantry and cried at the end of my first homeschooling day? Yeah. It happened. So, don't get too stuck on methodology at first. You can start a new homeschooled child with an unschooling approach, where you allow the child to pick what they want and learn naturally, until you become accustomed to homeschooling. You can always adjust what works for your child later. I'm over five years into homeschooling and I still adjust throughout the year.

So how do you get started?

My recommendation is that you do online research for different homeschooling methods and then start with the one that sounds most like how your child learns (or best fits your family). Don't be afraid to try out a method for a couple of weeks or less . . . or more, sometimes it will quickly become clear that a method is or isn't working, while other times it may take a little longer. Just know that you can stop or change directions if a specific style doesn't work for your family.

Also, if you change methods or styles, don't perceive that as a failure. You want to be sure that you are creating the best learning environment for your child, and switching up homeschooling methods that are not working is part of that. See it as a positive instead of a negative: *I get to choose exactly what works for my child, including the ability to adjust throughout the year!*

Another thing you can do is just start learning and then ease your way into a method. For example, if your child loves cheetahs, build some learning around that topic that includes writing and math and art (or whatever). Approaching homeschooling this way, especially in the beginning, will give you a little time to observe how your homeschooler learns best and then you can match a method to your learner.

Homeschool Homework 6

Research One or Two Methods Further

Search online for "homeschool methods" and do some reading on the different topics. Remember, I just gave you a quick overview of a few methods earlier, so you'll definitely need to research more. If you saw a method that piqued your interest, take a moment to research it and learn more about it now. Don't forget to add notes to your journal or notebook so that you can refer back to it later.

Myth #7: "I'm not sure if I want to homeschool all the way through high school, so I don't think I should start."

One of the biggest mistakes new homeschooling parents make is going into it with an "all or nothing" mentality. If you think about it, that's a lot of pressure: "I'm going to start something I've never done before and I'm going to make it work for *years* no matter what."

Yikes.

Some people go into homeschooling knowing that they will only homeschool during the elementary school years. They then plan to enroll in a traditional school during the middle or high school years. That is one way to go.

Personally, I went into homeschooling with the mentality of "we will continue to do this until it doesn't work for us." That way of thinking gave me a lot of (mental) room to fail and forgive myself. It also gave my daughter the ability to open a dialogue with me about traditional school if she becomes interested in that.

A couple of years ago, when my daughter was seven, she did come to me and inquire about school. She was curious about it. After some discussion, I found out that she was most curious about riding a bus and about what lockers looked like . . . not actually *going* to school. So, I found a bus driver to let us tour a school bus. Later, when we were at a public high school for a play, I showed her the lockers and talked to her about how they worked. Turned out, it wasn't that she wanted to go to traditional school, it was just that she was curious about a couple of the processes that she saw on a television show. Since then, she hasn't brought up traditional school and, so far, homeschooling has worked for us. However, I'm never going to close that door of allowing her to discuss her educational options with me. I still check in with her on occasion to see how she feels about homeschooling versus traditional school.

The truth is this: you don't have to have it all figured out from the get-go. *Really.* You don't have to know if you will homeschool during your child's entire school years. You are allowed to change your mind. You will change curricula and schedules and even methods. You will fail. You will succeed. You will tweak and plan and then tweak again and plan again until it works for your family. Again, this flexibility is one of the greatest benefits of homeschooling! There will be days when you go to sleep thinking, "This is the most amazing journey ever!" There will also be days when you go to sleep thinking, "What just happened today?" and feel like the biggest failure. These thoughts and experiences are normal; so don't go into it thinking you need to have it all figured out all day, every day, for the rest of your child's education starting at day one.

If you're interested in homeschooling, then start homeschooling. The end. The rest will fall into place as you go along. (You have to trust me on this.)

Homeschool Homework 7

Write down your vision of homeschooling. Do you want to homeschool all the way through high school? Is it something you just want to do for preschool and kindergarten? Maybe you have no idea right now? Then, take a moment to ask your family members how they envision homeschooling. You might be surprised how your spouse, partner, or even kids answer the question. It may also give you some insight for long-term homeschool planning. Be sure to document any relevant information in your notebook or journal.

JACQUELINE WILSON

Myth #8: "Homeschooling is just regular school, but at home in your pajamas."

Homeschooling is not just regular schooling, but—happily—you *can* do it in your pajamas if you want!

Let's first tackle the "regular schooling" part. Homeschooling is not "regular schooling" or a mirror of public school. In many states, parents get to choose their own homeschool curricula and method of learning, which can vary greatly from what is being taught in public school. Even if homeschool families live in a state where they have to follow a state-required curriculum, homeschool parents can still provide learning in the environment of their choice and supplement learning how they want. So, homeschooling is not at all like regular schooling. Every homeschooler's schedule and learning and experience is different.

However, the part about the pajamas can be true. There have been many blistery winter days where we didn't have to get out of the house and my daughter did her studies in her pajamas. Does it impede her learning? Heck no! She's comfortable and she gets to learn while being comfortable. I would say sorry, but I'm not sorry at all that homeschoolers get the benefit of this comfort.

Homeschooling Versus Schooling At Home

This is a great place to talk about the difference between *homeschooling* and *schooling at home*. **Homeschooling** is learning at home, where the parent takes control of the child's education. Homeschooling is parent-directed and parent-led, and generally learning is done at the child's pace. Depending on the state where you live, homeschooling may include using a state specified curriculum, but many homeschooling states allow parents to choose the curriculum for their children.

Schooling at home is often also (mistakenly) called homeschooling; however, it is very different. Schooling at home–also called virtual public school, virtual school, or tuition-free school–is following a public school or an educational institute's state-required curriculum at home. These programs are usually offered through public schools or through state-approved programs and often require students to participate in the state's standardized testing and meet other state school requirements. A student works at the predetermined pace set by the school, generally through an online program, and submits work and examinations. The student is basically participating in public school, but just doing the work from home.

Also, don't make the mistake of thinking that all online programs are public school programs. Just because a program or course is performed online doesn't necessarily mean that it's a state controlled program. There are many independent homeschooling programs and courses that are offered online and have nothing to do with state mandated curricula.

While homeschooling and schooling at home are both great options, do not be confused if you are new to this subject. Homeschooling gives you control over your child's learning, while schooling at home follows a state program just like public school. If you want total control over your homeschooling and your child's learning, signing up for a virtual school at home (that is funded by, or affiliated with, public schools) will not offer that, so be sure you understand the program before committing.

Homeschool Homework 8

Take a moment to search online for "virtual public schools." Pick one or two of these public programs and take a look at the websites and information. Then, check out time4learning.com, which is one web-based, independent homeschool program offered online. This will help you understand the differences between virtual public school (schooling at home) and homeschooling online. If you see any programs that are of interest to you, jot them down in your notebook or journal.

JACQUELINE WILSON

Myth #9: "You have to keep your kids inside during school hours or child protective services will visit."

This is *still* a discussion that I frequently hear in homeschooling groups: "Should we keep our kids indoors during traditional school hours?"

To be honest, I don't even worry about this. If my daughter wants to take a break from her studies and play in the backyard at 10 a.m. for a little while, I allow that. If we want to go out to lunch on a school day in between our home studies and the classes we have out of house, we go to lunch in a public place. *(Gasp!)* If I need to run to the grocery store on the way to one of her outside classes, I do that too.

I don't worry about being out during "school hours," but we do get some questions when we are out. If you're new to homeschooling, you should be prepared for that. It's not unusual for a waitress, or a store clerk, or the librarian to say to my daughter, "Oh! Are you out of school today?" When my daughter answers, "I'm homeschooled," we often get a familiar look that implies, "Oh, so you do nothing during the day." So, the judgment is still there, even today, in a state like mine where there is a large homeschooling population. However, we are doing nothing wrong and, more importantly, nothing illegal.

So, don't feel the need to quarantine your child during traditional school hours. Instead, grow a thick skin and know that some people are going to question and judge. Just be sure to understand the child protective service and truancy laws and regulations for your state. There might be a case where someone–typically a neighbor that may regularly see your child outside during traditional school hours–will contact child protective services and file a complaint that your child is not in school. In many cases, child protective services do not have to be allowed into your home without a warrant. Keep in mind, there are some exceptions, like if they feel the child is being abused or is in danger. Become familiar with those laws in your state so that you're covered and know how to respond if you ever do get a visit.

Homeschool Homework 9

Read through *Child Protective Services Investigations* found at:

http://www.hslda.org/docs/nche/Issues/P/Privacy_CPS.asp

Also, consider making a list of neighbors or other people who you may want to alert about your homeschooling. Many times, it is a simple misunderstanding about your child being home during school hours. If you bring up your intention to homeschool (or that you are homeschooling) in a discussion with your neighbors, it lets them know that your family is not breaking truancy laws.

JACQUELINE WILSON

Myth #10: "It's too expensive to homeschool."

Homeschooling can be costly, but not so expensive that you cannot do it. Traditional schooling and associated extracurricular activities can also be expensive. Just like any facet of raising a family, your expenses will be determined by your choices. For homeschooling, it will include decisions like what curriculum you use and what activities your kids are involved in outside of the home. If your homeschooled kid is involved in a lot of extra classes, your expenses will be higher (just like if a traditionally schooled kid is in a lot of extracurricular activities).

Multiple homeschool sources list that the average cost of homeschooling a child the first year is around $600 to $900. Your first year will probably be the most expensive because you are just figuring it all out. You may have a few trial and error purchases (curricula, books, online classes, etc.) before you find what really works for you. (By the way, just as an interesting comparison, a 2014 study reported that one year of public school can cost the system an average of $11,009 per student.)

One of the biggest expenses you will probably incur as a homeschooling family will be curricula and at-home courses. There are boxed curricula or online courses available that will make your homeschooling life easier. However, these curricula and courses can run into a few hundred dollars for each kid or learning level (at the most expensive end of the spectrum). On the other hand, there are many free or cheap resources where you can find homeschool curricula, study units, worksheets, and online reading that help keep homeschooling expenses down. (Repeat after me: the library is your friend!)

The next biggest (or equal) expense will be the number and type of classes you take outside of the home. We try to do a mix of paid classes (music, Spanish, swim) and free classes, like those offered through a museum or a library. Like we discussed earlier, many organizations today have recognized the growing homeschooling movement and have added free or cheap homeschool classes to their offerings. If you don't see a class at one of your favorite places, ask for it! A mom in one of our homeschooling classes asked a local gourmet grocery store to add affordable homeschool cooking classes to their roster of class offerings. They listened and now it is a very popular class—which is a win for both them and us!

The cost of homeschooling will depend completely on how you homeschool and what your child wants to be involved in outside of the home. You will need to budget what works for your family.

Homeschool Homework 10

Refer back to the classes you listed in Homeschool Homework 3. Review the classes and costs and give some consideration about how they will fit into your schedule and budget. Document your thoughts in your notebook or journal. If you have the *It's Homeschooling! Journal,* use the blank activity calendars to do a mock up of what your homeschooling week might look like with the extra courses or activities outside of the home.

JACQUELINE WILSON

Myth #11: "Homeschool kids can't play sports."

You may be surprised to learn that just because a child is homeschooled it doesn't necessarily mean that he or she is excluded from participating in public school sports. (I know, crazy!) However, each state has the ability to determine if homeschoolers are eligible to participate in public school sports.

For example, according to the Homeschool Legal Defense Association (HSLDA), Arizona statute states, "Homeschooled students are allowed to participate in the public schools' interscholastic activities 'in the same manner' as pupils who are enrolled in the public schools." However, there are other states that prohibit homeschoolers from participating in public school sports. California statute specifically states, "California Interscholastic Federation prohibits homeschoolers from playing on public school teams."

So, why did some public schools start allowing homeschoolers the ability to participate in school sports?

Enter: Tim Tebow Law

By the year 2014, 28 states had adopted "Equal Access Athletics" bills. They are commonly referred to as the "Tim

Tebow Law."

Tim Tebow was a Florida homeschooler who played public school football. He went on to play college football and then to have a successful career in the National Football League (NFL). Tim Tebow's success paved the way for a widespread review of athletics in order to allow homeschoolers to play sports in public school districts.

Each state has different regulations regarding homeschoolers participating in public school sport activities, so be sure you check the information for your state. Even if your state does not allow homeschoolers to participate in public school sports, there are plenty of other places to get homeschooled kids involved. Check your local YMCA or other community sports complexes. Again, don't be afraid to ask a school or organization to add a homeschooling sports class to their offerings. The swim class my daughter attends is at a high school that has one of the best competitive swim teams in the state. They started offering homeschool swim classes during the day when the school's pool is not being used by the school or swim team. So, we receive the same instruction from excellent coaches, only with smaller classes at more affordable rates.

If you are only looking for a physical education class to keep your kids active, there are typically plenty of those in any state. We were fortunate enough to find a free homeschool physical education class at a local church once per week with a former physical education teacher and soccer coach. You will just need to do some research for your area.

Homeschool Homework 11

Talk with your children about what sports they may be interested in as part of homeschooling. Review the homeschooling sports regulations for your state's public schools at

http://www.hslda.org/docs/nche/Issues/E/Equal_Access.pdf

If your state does not allow homeschool students to participate in public school sports, search online for sports classes or homeschool physical education classes in your area (search: *homeschool physical education [your city, state]*). Be sure to note any classes of interest in your notebook or journal so that you have it all in one place when you're ready to sign up.

JACQUELINE WILSON

Myth #12: "You cannot work or contribute financially to your family if you homeschool."
(Or: "I don't have time for homeschooling.")

It's true, almost all homeschooling families have at least one parent at home taking on the full-time responsibilities of homeschooling, but that does not mean that you can't work and homeschool. As I mentioned before, homeschooling is not for the faint of heart. Homeschooling is all encompassing and that includes taking up a majority of your day. With all of that said, there are those who work and contribute financially to the family—even single parents— while successfully homeschooling!

Some homeschool families have both parents who work, and some single parent families work outside of the home while still homeschooling. How homeschooling works for these families will depend on what kind of job the parents have and how flexible it is. For instance, maybe one parent works during the day and one works at night. The day working parent may homeschool from 7 a.m. to 9 a.m. and then hand off the kids to a caregiver or a co-op class. The second (late working parent) may then take care of additional homeschool activities or pick up the kids from their co-op class or caregiver. There are also single parents who work daytime shifts and then homeschool in the afternoon or evenings. Maybe the parent works at night and homeschools in the morning or during the day. We have friends where one parent works only on the weekends, leaving them both at home to homeschool during the week.

I recently had a discussion on the Homeschool Super Freak Facebook page with a homeschool mom who said her kids are natural night owls. She works part-time during the morning hours, and then she homeschools her kids in the afternoon and early evening hours and it works really well for their natural body clocks.

I happen to have a writing and consulting business that I started about seven years before my daughter was born. By the time she came along, the business was established. When I started homeschooling, I told my clients about my decision and they were all supportive of working around my schedule. I've even taken my daughter to business meetings! (I call her "the closer.") There are also occasional times during a homeschooling day that I take a conference call or have to spend time on an immediate business issue. During that time, my daughter has independent projects she works on until we can resume our schedule. I spend evenings, the time my daughter is in outside classes, or even on the weekends, following up on business responsibilities or working. It's a juggling act and it certainly is not easy, but it can be done if you're committed. You can make time to homeschool no matter your schedule, you financial needs, or your family dynamic.

As your children get older, they become more autonomous and take more control of their own learning. You can reserve teaching times together for when it fits around your work schedule. During the other times, your child can spend time completing online classes, working through a workbook, or even completing a curriculum with another family member or caregiver.

Juggling homeschooling and working will be hard. You will be tired. There will be days that you will question your decision. (We all do, even those who don't work!) But, you can make time to homeschool, or work and homeschool, if you're committed to the process of taking control of your child's education. (By the way, this is where a homeschool support group comes in really handy!)

Homeschool Homework 12

If you don't currently have a monthly budget, spend some time determining your monthly expenses. If you need to work while homeschooling, how will you handle your expenses? What can be cut out from your expenses? What would a normal homeschool/work day look like for your family? What are the costs of the extra classes outside of the home? Brainstorm on the topic and document it in your journal or notebook.

Myth #13: "Kids need the structure of a traditional school to be successful."

Clearly I don't agree with this statement, so I am a little biased. Thankfully, you don't have to listen to my opinions because there are plenty of articles, studies, research, and information out there to support the fact that kids do not necessarily need structure like a regimented public school system to be successful in education and then later in their lives. An author on Education.com writes, "Preschoolers need unstructured time to learn how things work, solve problems, use their imaginations, and practice skills they've recently learned. And most of all, they need time to just be kids!" There is a great deal of learning that takes place when a child, even an older child, is allowed free learning and free play.

Let's take a look at a more relaxed educational model, which is now being studied by some educators across the world. Students in Finland have consistently scored high on international tests, including in math and science. However, their schools run completely opposite of traditional schools in the United States.

In Finland, they don't start formal education until age seven and they place a high emphasis on play and exploring during that time. The country also ends school at the U.S.

equivalent of ninth grade. At that point, students can choose their own track, which includes vocational school, upper secondary school, or they can venture out into the workforce. Reports from Finnish schools state that only about 5 percent of students choose to work at that point in time.

A school day for Finnish students starts between 9 and 10 a.m. and ends around 2 to 3 p.m. The late start is based on research that shows students, especially adolescents, need more sleep. And—this was really mind-blowing— the school days don't start and end at the same time each day! The days are flexible and changing based on what is scheduled for the day (which is generally how homeschooling is, too).

The Finnish school day includes three to four different classes that last a little over an hour each. The day is also peppered with 10 to 20 minute breaks that give both students and teachers an opportunity to rest between topics, refresh, and be better prepared for the next topic. (What a concept!)

Teachers in Finland spend around four hours or less in the classroom each day. Conversely, teachers in the United States spend at least six hours in the classroom each day, not counting preparation time. In Finland, the students keep the same teacher for three to six years, allowing teachers to adjust learning styles for each child . . . much like we would in homeschooling!

Oh! And guess what else? In Finland, there is no pressure for state testing (unlike how so much of the public school curriculum is based around state testing in the United States) and there is a more relaxed curriculum timeline. If a teacher feels that more time is needed on a topic, he or she simply spends more time. There is no pressure to push forward into the next topic in order to get all the state requirements completed by the end of the year. One U.S. teacher reported that a Finnish school where she had observed offered math class only one time each week. Yet, Finnish schools consistently have some of the highest math scores in the entire world. The students in Finland hardly have any homework and, if they do, it is not more than a half an hours worth of work. Also, assignments are often not even graded, yet students still do them and out-perform other countries.

One last thing that Finland is implementing: they are studying events and phenomena in an interdisciplinary format instead of breaking them down into individual subjects, which is very similar to the way that topic- or project-based learning takes place in homeschooling. In this style of learning, you choose a topic and then incorporate all subjects into that one topic. Remember our earlier example of a homeschooler who was interested in cheetahs? The homeschooling parent builds learning around that one topic, incorporating math, reading, art and more around the topic of cheetahs. For reading, maybe your child reads a book about cheetahs. For math, your child could calculate the distance that cheetahs run or determine how much faster or slower cheetahs run than other animals. For art, maybe your child could paint a picture of a cheetah after studying the anatomy of one. That is exactly how Finland, one of the most successful educational countries in the world, is now moving toward educating students! Marjo Kyllonen, from the Department of Education in Helsinki, said, "There are schools that are teaching in the old-fashioned way which was of benefit in the beginning of the 1900s—but the needs are not the same, and we need something fit for the 21st century."

Why am I sharing all of this information about Finland and what does it have to do with homeschooling? Because as I've been reading more about the Finnish education model, one thing keeps jumping out to me: it is very similar to how we homeschool—the same teacher for years, the ability to set your own pace for learning, the idea where we allow our children to feel completely comfortable with a topic before moving on, the differing schedules for each day, the no homework policy, the more breaks and rest and time for free play and exploring, the project-based or topic-based learning—all of this is a model that is proving to be successful in Finland. This is exactly the opposite of how the United States currently approaches education. This should have homeschoolers excited since we operate in much the same way as Finland and they are consistently out-scoring the rest of the world!

So, the next time someone mentions that kids need the "structure" of a traditional school, point them to Finland and their test scores . . . and then take great pleasure in comparing how the school schedule and structure in Finland is very similar to how homeschooling is scheduled and structured.

Homeschool Homework 13

The most relaxed method of homeschooling is the unstructured style of unschooling. Search online for *unschooling* and read more about this style of homeschooling.

Then, head over to Facebook.com and search Facebook for *Unschooling* or *Autonomous Homeschoolers*. Request to join the group. Once in the group, interact with some of the members there. Be upfront if you are researching homeschooling for your family or would like to know the pros and cons of an unstructured philosophy like unschooling. In your journal or notebook, write down the points and comments about unschooling that stand out to you. Is this style of homeschooling something you would consider? If you already homeschool in another style, would you like to add one day each week of unschooling? Do you believe this style would be better for your family?

Myth #14: "Homeschool kids have a hard time getting accepted into college."

This is an exciting time because, overall, colleges are happy to accept homeschoolers that meet the same enrollment requirements as traditionally schooled students. The problems seem to stem mostly from some colleges not understanding state homeschooling laws and inaccurately requiring homeschoolers to provide a GED, which has led to confusion and misinformation circulating that it is hard for homeschoolers to get into colleges and universities. For example, the Homeschool Legal Defense Association (HSLDA) discusses an issue where two Florida homeschooled students were told that they needed GEDs if they wanted to attend the local community college. Once the HSLDA contacted the college and made them aware of the homeschooling laws, the homeschooled students were admitted to the college with no issues.

Ivy league colleges and many others are also starting to see the value of a homeschool education. You may remember a *Boston Magazine* feature about a homeschooler admitted to Harvard just a couple of years ago. The *Business Insider* writes that it's not the homeschooling part that makes colleges actively recruit homeschool students.

Instead, the publication states that it's the freedom of homeschoolers to add a wide variety of learning to their daily schedules that are outside of a rigid classroom environment that make them so appealing. In addition to academics, colleges and universities also look at a student's community service and extra curricular activities—all things that homeschoolers are often involved in regularly. "The high achievement level of homeschoolers is readily recognized by recruiters from some of the best colleges in the nation," education expert Dr. Susan Berry said, as reported by *Business Insider*. The publication also reports, "Away from the standardized tests and rigid schedules in public education, kids can let their creative sides flourish, learn about the world they live in, and, when it's time, earn acceptance into the best colleges in the world." (We couldn't agree more.)

So, how does your homeschooler get a diploma from homeschool so that he or she can apply to college? You can make a diploma from your homeschool that can be submitted to colleges (for real). There are even software programs that help you to track and create a transcript of your homeschooler's work that can be submitted to colleges and universities . . . just like in traditional school!

Homeschool Homework 14

Spend some time looking through the links below of colleges

that have a history of accepting homeschoolers. If you're at this stage, be sure to document in your journal or notebook if there are any institutes you think your child may be interested in so that you can do further research.

http://learninfreedom.org/colleges-home-schooled-students.html

http://www.thebestschools.org/blog/2012/06/24/25-colleges-homeschool-graduates/

http://www.bestvalueschools.com/colleges-for-homeschoolers/

http://www.homeschoolfacts.com/homeschool-friendly-colleges.html

JACQUELINE WILSON

Myth #15: "It's important for kids to experience real life and they just can't get that from homeschooling."

Um, what?

That is actually my educated response when people say something like this because it is so perplexing. A comment like this means that the person making the statement really has no idea about the process of homeschooling and has succumbed to that void of myths and misinformation circulating out there. If anything, many homeschoolers are experiencing much more "real life" than those students who are in a classroom setting at a desk for hours on end each day. In fact, homeschooling often creates well-rounded students with fantastic life experiences. The *Business Insider* supports this by writing, "Contrary to popular belief, homeschoolers are not shut-ins. Research suggests that homeschooled children actually gain closer ties to their community, relating to people outside of their grade level. Homeschoolers learn to become active participants in their neighborhoods and soak up the etiquette of adult life in the process."

One of the things that many homeschooling families work on (including myself) right alongside academic studies is a focus on real life skills like cleaning, laundry, cooking, time management, problem-solving, conflict resolution, money management, and much, much more. These skills are just as important as academic skills and may be an area that traditional schools are falling short. Did you read that article a few years ago where an ivy-league school counselor said that college students are showing up meeting the academic requirements, but are failing miserably at life skills? Yeah, I don't want that for my child (and I'm pretty sure you don't either). I want a child who not only excels academically, but can also manage her money, do her laundry, cook, and take care of other daily living responsibilities.

Another way homeschooling families provide life experience is through travel. Many homeschooling parents work hard to expose their children to travel and culture regularly, which you cannot get a lot of by sitting in a classroom five days each week for the majority of a year. Travel is an important learning component for many homeschoolers and holds many benefits. A child can easily learn a new language by being immersed in a new culture. They will be able to explore museums, history, and artifacts of different societies. Also, children will learn important skills like how to adapt, accept, and be patient. There are so many ways that travel engages and excites a child. Dr. Margot Sunderland, child psychotherapist, says, "An enriched environment offers new experiences that are strong in combined social, physical, cognitive, and sensory interaction."

Related Myth: "Homeschoolers can't successfully contribute to society."

One day, I posted a graphic on the Homeschool Super Freak Facebook page. It compared kids sitting in a classroom learning about nature to homeschooled kids outside observing and learning about nature. Seems innocent enough, right? Not long after, someone (presumably a non-homeschooler) commented that the graphic was untrue and that homeschoolers could never contribute to society without structure and without being able to socialize with other kids.

Remember a few chapters ago when I referenced The National Home Education Resource Institute (NHERI) study that said homeschoolers participate in multiple social activities outside the home and that "78 percent of high school home learners were employed with paying jobs, while a majority engaged in volunteering and community service"? Getting jobs and volunteering seems to be a valid way of contributing to society, right?

We make volunteering and giving back a regular part of our homeschooling. It's an added benefit of having a flexible schedule that you can fit volunteering and giving back to the community wherever it fits into your schedule. Maybe your child likes gardening and you can find a community garden that needs help? Or, maybe you have an elderly neighbor who could use meals cooked by your homeschooler? Or, maybe you have a family of animal lovers and can volunteer together at a local animal shelter? Or, maybe you have a techy type kid who loves blogging or creating websites? There are even online volunteer opportunities, especially with nonprofit organizations, that would appreciate talents like that! There are so many opportunities for your homeschoolers to contribute to society and volunteering is such a great learning opportunity!

Oh, and one more thing. The day that person left the comment on the Homeschool Super Freak Facebook page, my daughter and I had just finished delivering bags of food and supplies to a food pantry because homeschoolers really do contribute to society . . . and your homeschooler will, too!

Homeschool Homework 15

How would you like to get your homeschooler involved in giving back to the community while homeschooling? Check out volunteer sites (like VolunteerMatch.org) or local churches or community bulletin boards and see if there are volunteer opportunities in your area. Also, ask friends, families, and other parents and homeschooling families about their local volunteering experiences. You may find great suggestions through them. Make sure to write down your ideas and findings in your journal or notebook.

JACQUELINE WILSON

Myth #16: "You will never know if your kids have learned anything."

Whenever a parent of a traditionally schooled child asks, "How will you know if your homeschooled child has learned anything?" I ask them, "Well, how do you know if your public school child has learned anything?" And, I'm genuinely interested in their answer. Most of the time the parents say, "Well, I get a report card."

Okay, then.

Unfortunately, a report card isn't always the best measurement of child's learning. DoSomething.org reports that one in four children in America do not know how to read. Reading Is Fundamental reports that, "93 million adults in the US read at or below the basic level needed to contribute successfully to society." Since the majority of people attend traditional school, it doesn't seem like we have found the best measurement tool. There has been a great deal of discussion in recent years about changing the way schools measure student progress (report cards, standardized tests, and more), but nothing has come to fruition within the educational system as a whole.

EducationWorld.com reported that report card "... inconsistencies often result in wide discrepancies in letter grade meaning, as classmates at different skill levels receive similar letter grades, while students in different classrooms, at the same skill level, receive different letter grades." It's a broken system. You don't have to believe me (or anyone else); instead you can do an internet search and do the research (or, better yet, talk to some public school teachers). There just isn't a good measurement system in place . . . yet. (But, I am hopeful!) So, I'm clearly not a fan of the answer, "I measure my child's progress by the report card."

So how do I measure progress? Instead of a report card, I measure my daughter's homeschool learning by being involved. Does her reading seem to be advancing? Is she further along in learning math then she was last month? Has she mastered more than one song on the piano from when she started three months ago? Measuring doesn't have to be standardized, like the all day tests many of us took when we were in public school. Instead, measurement can just be observing their progress (or lack of progress). Think of the way you knew your toddler was learning new things—one day he could crawl and a few weeks later he could walk. You just watched the natural progression of learning and knew. And, if you're exposing your children to new and challenging experiences that advance them to the next learning level, it's a safe bet that they're learning. You'll know this even without a report card.

Related Myth: "You will never be able to keep up with current educational requirements."

With all of that said, how do you know if your homeschooler is at the right learning stage for his or her age? In some states, you don't have a choice as a homeschooling parent. You may have to take standardized tests as a homeschool requirement and also follow specific curricula or subject requirements. (So, again, know your state's homeschool laws and reporting and testing requirements!) In other states, you have more flexibility and the understanding of where your homeschooled child is for his or her learning level will come from being involved and observing. It seems like an ambiguous answer, but it really does work this way. Additionally, you may use a curriculum or online course that provides feedback on advancement or measuring tools that allow you to see your child's progress.

Technically, I don't measure or grade my homeschooler. However, when preparing for an upcoming new year, I do review a few standards for my daughter's upcoming grade by researching our state standards for that grade and also searching educational sites online. I do this mainly to gain a starting point for building upon her studies for the year. If there are some things that she seems behind on compared to those standards, I will spend extra time on that topic. If she seems to be above the standards listed for her grade level, I bump her up a level or two so she can continue to be in a challenging learning environment.

Also—and maybe most importantly—you need to retrain yourself in the way that you think. Repeat after me (again): **homeschool is not traditional school.** Then keep repeating that mantra to yourself over and over again until you really start to let go of the traditional perspectives of schooling.

If you're not required by your state, then you don't need to give grades or measure results (unless you want to do so). Children will learn naturally on their own if you expose them to a variety of learning tools. By just following standards or measurements, you are not allowing your homeschooler to learn at his or her own pace or interests—which are some of the biggest advantages of homeschooling! You may find that your second grader is advancing quickly in reading, but needs to slow down and spend more time on math. This is naturally apparent as you work with your child during studies.

Lastly, if you're still intent on testing and measuring, there are ways you can do that during homeschooling. Use curricula or online courses that allow you to track progress. Educational websites (think: math, spelling, and reading games) often allow a parent account to oversee the progress in the games. My homeschooler has a reading app on her tablet. Each week I get an email that updates me on how many pages she's read and what books she chose to read. She also does math games on a website that gives me access to what she's learning and what she needs to work on for specific areas. There are plenty of ways to keep track of what a homeschooled child is learning and his or her progress.

If you're looking for an overall progress report, there are organizations that provide independent progress measurements, like the standardized testing found in traditional schools. And, most of these can be completed online right from the comfort of your home.

Related Myth: "You will never know what grade your kid is in."

Some homeschooling parents have an inside joke that our kids get nervous when someone asks them, "What grade are you in?" When people ask our homeschooled kids their grade, sometimes they get a panicked look on their faces and then look at us (the parents) with wide eyes. That's because some homeschooling families don't make a big deal about grade level. Sure, we know what grade they're in. It might take us a moment to remember (just like it takes me a moment to remember my daughter's age sometimes), but we know. Instead, some homeschooling families pace learning based on the needs of each specific child. (Remember, this flexibility and control are some of the biggest benefits of homeschooling!) For example, you might have a homeschooler who would be in third grade according to traditional school. However, she may have a fifth grade math level, fourth grade reading level, and a second grade spelling level. The great thing about homeschooling is that this child's parent can then provide more challenging lessons in math and reading where she is excelling, while also spending more time on spelling where she is having a little more trouble.

In most traditional schools, all students in a specific grade are generally learning on the same level. At some point, the teacher must move forward in the studies, no matter where students are, so that all of the state requirements for the school year can be met. A benefit of homeschooling is that you have the opportunity to advance or slow down based on how your child is learning. So, if a homeschooler looks confused when asked what grade he or she is in, it's not that they don't know. The homeschoolers just may not know how to answer because "I'm in third grade, but I'm in fifth grade math, fourth grade reading, and second grade spelling" seems like a lot to explain.

Related Myth: "Your child will fall behind and they will never be able to catch up again."

No matter if a child is homeschooled or traditionally schooled, chances are there is a point during school studies that he or she may fall behind. A 2016 *Kids Count* report released by the Annie E. Casey Foundation revealed that in 2015 there were 65 percent of publicly schooled fourth graders who were not proficient in reading and 68 percent of publicly schooled eighth graders who were not proficient in math. Additionally, a 2012 to 2013 study indicated that 18 percent of high school kids did not graduate on time. Lastly, a 2012 report, *Getting Students on Track to College and Career Readiness: How Many Catch Up from Far Behind?*, revealed that kids who are behind in grades four and eight have only a 1 in 3 chance of being ready for college or a job by the end of high school.

As you can see, falling behind isn't an unusual thing, no matter where the learning takes place. However, what differentiates homeschool and traditional school for this topic is that traditional schools must stay on track, pushing forward in order to meet state-mandated requirements, which can leave struggling students behind. Conversely, even homeschooling families who must follow a state curriculum can take more time to learn the topics their child is struggling with and can also spend the extra time or resources within their normal homeschooling day to help their child catch up.

Homeschool Homework 16

Search the internet for homeschool testing requirements for your state. Then, give some thought to whether or not you want to test your homeschooler to measure progress. (It's OK if you don't know yet!) Ask yourself: *Will I measure progress? If so, how?*

Also, take time to search the internet for phrases like *homeschool progress tests* to see what is available. Be sure to document your notes, thoughts, and findings in your journal or notebook. Highlight your state requirements so you don't forget!

If you have a homeschooler that falls in the preschool to fifth grade range, visit PBS.org to get an overview of what standard learning levels are like for these grades. Visit:

http://www.pbs.org/parents/education/going-to-school/

Myth #17: "I don't have the patience to homeschool."

This is a common one that homeschooling families hear quite often. A parent will tell you that they are not patient enough to homeschool so they would never even consider it. Here's my confession: I'm not the most patient person, so I get it when people say this. Honestly, it was a concern of mine before I started homeschooling. "Would I *really* have enough patience to do this?"

If this is one of your concerns, or something you're hearing from others, think about it this way: how do impatient people do anything in life? How do they patiently stand in line, or take four-hour tests, or sit in a college class for an hour, or wait during an appointment to get their driver's license updated? Impatient people just *do it* because it is part of life. And, homeschooling is no different. There will be days when you will be impatient with your homeschooler (and your homeschooler will be impatient with you) just the same as there are days when parents of traditionally schooled kids will be impatient with their kids during homework time or doing anything else as a family.

Related Myth: "Being with my kid that much will make me insane!"

This is an interesting one: some parents reveal to homeschooling parents that they could never be with their children all day long. Whenever a parent says this, I assume they really mean that they do not have the patience for it.

Look, your kids are going to make you crazy some days (and you're going to make them crazy), no matter if you homeschool or you send your kids to another type of school. That's just the nature of being a parent and it really doesn't have anything to do with homeschooling.

And about that "no patience and insane" thing: the nature of a homeschool schedule is generally more relaxed. So, once you find your groove, I think you'll be surprised at how it's not as stressful as you might think. I'm betting that you'll even enjoy the majority of the learning time with your child!

Related Myth: "My kids will hate each other after spending all that time together!"

Show me a family where the siblings don't argue and I'll show you . . . well, nothing, because that kind of family doesn't exist. Kids argue. They get on each other's nerves (heck, they get on our nerves and vice versa). That bickering doesn't necessarily increase or decrease because of homeschooling. It is just part of a normal family dynamic.

So, do homeschooled siblings get on each other's nerves? Probably. Do traditionally schooled siblings get on each other's nerves? Probably.

Also, remember that a homeschool day isn't made up of just you and your kids locked in a room at home with their faces in books, never going outside or interacting or doing anything else. A typical homeschool day (or week) will probably include some at-home study, as well as some outside-the-home activities. Your kids will have plenty of time working on their own solo projects, as well as attending separate classes, camps, activities, and play dates that will diffuse the sibling spats. If all else fails, send them outside into the yard or take them to a park to release some of that energy!

Related Myth: "Your children are better behaved than mine, so I can't homeschool."

Um, nope. That old saying "Kids will be kids!" is out there for a reason.

There's a myth that homeschooled kids are better behaved. Most homeschooled kids are pretty great, but they are still kids. Homeschooling parents face much of the same challenges that other parents face! Homeschooled kids have days when they're extremely well behaved and then there are days when things are a little off . . . just like anyone. Homeschooled kids are not abnormally amazing, the same way that homeschooling parents are not saints.

(But we are pretty great, huh?)

Homeschool Homework 17

Take a moment to consider your patience level. When are you most impatient? Is it when you wake up in the morning and you are feeling hectic with the rush of a new day, or is it when you're tired? Is it when you've had unrealistic expectations that don't get met? Is it when you're feeling pulled in too many different directions?

In your journal or notebook, document the situations that make you the most impatient. Then, become aware of how you feel when impatience is approaching. Do you tense up? Do you feel anger rising? Do you start to clinch your teeth or hands, or do you yell? Do you shut down and just want to nap? Document how you feel when becoming impatient to make yourself aware of when you're losing patience. Then, develop a practice that you can follow when this happens.

For example:

1. I will breathe deeply 10 times.
2. I will take a break and walk away from the situation in order to force myself to slow down.

3. In extreme cases, I will [insert something that calms you . . . pet the dog, take a walk, watch mindless TV, etc.].

Dealing with impatience takes conscious effort and practice! But, losing patience happens to the best of us. You need to give yourself a break when you have that impatient *snap*! (It *will* happen.)

JACQUELINE WILSON

Myth #18: "Homeschoolers hate when you ask them questions."

A friend, whose kids go to traditional public school, once said to me, "I'm afraid to ask homeschooling parents questions. It doesn't seem like they are open to talking about it." Since that day, I've given that statement a great deal of thought and I've come to this conclusion: it's not that homeschooling parents don't like to talk about homeschooling (many of us do!) or hate answering questions (many of us don't mind!), it's just that we may be skeptical of the motive. Homeschooling families get so much judgment that some of us may be a little on edge when answering questions, and that may come across as being closed off and unwilling to discuss homeschooling.

Many people that we have met have a natural curiosity about homeschooling and it's interesting to talk with them about it. However, some people ask homeschooling families questions just as an opening to share their judgments about homeschooling. It's something that happens to homeschooling families on a regular basis—not just once or twice a month, but sometimes as much as several times each day depending on where we are . . . and it can be exhausting. That may be the undercurrent that some people are picking up on when they think that homeschooling parents do not want to discuss homeschooling. It's not that we don't want to talk about homeschooling, it's that we have probably been burned before and may be more cautious about being open when we first meet new people.

In reality, most homeschool families don't hate to answer questions about homeschooling. Actually, we like to talk about it to people who are legitimately interested. (I like to hear about traditional school methods as much as I like to hear about homeschool methods!) However, most of us are too emotionally exhausted to engage in judgmental conversations, so it might come across as cold if we suspect that motives are not pure in learning about our lives.

Homeschool Homework 18

Do you have a trusted friend who traditionally schools his or her kids? If so, open an honest dialogue with them about homeschooling and see if they have any questions. This will help you understand how to respond to questions others have about your homeschooling lifestyle. Be sure to write down any of the interesting questions that come up in your journal or notebook and also document how you answered them.

You can also head over to a homeschooling Facebook group (like the Homeschool Super Freak Facebook page) and ask the homeschooling parents there how they handle some of the questions that they are asked about homeschooling. It will be interesting to hear responses and viewpoints from different people!

JACQUELINE WILSON

Myth #19: "Something terrible must have happened to you in school for you to choose homeschooling."

I have a secret: nothing traumatic happened to me when I attended public school. Let's face it, if you attended traditional school, some of it was probably awesome and some of it was probably downright awful. This may or may not affect your decision to homeschool.

My experience in traditional public school was fine and normal like many others. I had some really high highs as well as some completely mortifying moments, like almost everyone who attended public school. However, my reason for homeschooling had very little to do with my experiences in school. (High school peer groups can be scary though, so that was on my mind.) Instead, my decision was mainly based on the fact that I thought I could provide my daughter with an educational experience filled with a large mix of things that catered to her interests better than a public school.

Choosing homeschooling solely because the parents had a terrible school experience probably pertains only to a small portion of homeschooling families. I have spoken to homeschoolers who have decided to homeschool for this reason, stating that they do not want their children exposed to the same negative experiences. However, the vast majority of homeschoolers have other reasons for homeschooling.

Related Myth: "Oh, you must live in a really bad school district if you're homeschooling!"

I happened to live in one of the best school district in our state, so this reason does not pertain to me either. I often get "Why would you homeschool? You live in a great school district!" when I first meet people. But, being in a great school district still did not make me want to stop homeschooling. And, I've yet to meet a homeschool parent who has listed "bad school district" as a reason for homeschooling.

However, living in a poor school district may be the reason for some homeschool families. Like we learned earlier, a 2012 National Household Education Survey (NHES) revealed that nine in 10 homeschooling parents chose homeschooling because they had a concern about the local school system. That was 91 percent of the parents surveyed who picked this as one of the reasons that they homeschooled, but 25 percent listed it as the most important reason. So, the majority of homeschooling families do not homeschool based necessarily on their past experiences, but instead homeschool based on the current state of the educational system. The statistics from the study might not necessarily mean that a family lives in a "bad school district." Instead, it could mean that the parents don't agree with the current educational system as a whole.

Homeschool Homework 19

Reflect on your reason for homeschooling. Revisit your journal notes from Homework 4. Are any past negative school or social experiences affecting your reasons to homeschool? Be sure to write them down in your journal or notebook.

JACQUELINE WILSON

Myth #20: "I don't have room in my house for a classroom so I can't homeschool."

Many people think that they need a large, empty room to create the homeschool classroom of their dreams (like the amazing craft rooms you see on all those renovation television shows). In reality, you don't need an extra room or a huge amount of space. Instead, you just need a designated area to keep your homeschool books and supplies organized. This can be a closet, bookshelves in the kids' rooms, an area in the garage, or just about anywhere—no matter if you live in an apartment, a super small condo, a fun farmhouse, or a sprawling mansion.

We have lived in two different homes since we've been homeschooling. In our first home, we had an entire extra room that the previous owners put in just to serve as their sitting room. Although it didn't have a door, it made for an amazing homeschool classroom. We had enough room for a huge craft table, two desks, four bookshelves, a reading corner, a toy chest, and still plenty of open floor space for activities and hanging out on floor pillows. It was a great space and it was nice to have the books and supplies organized and easy to view, but we homeschooled all over our house and not just in that room. Over time we homeschooled less in that amazing dedicated room and more around the house in different areas.

For the next house, we downsized and didn't have an extra bedroom for our homeschool classroom. We instead used an open space at the front of our house (right by the front door for all to see . . . *yikes*!). I think the room was supposed to be a formal living room. It isn't the most ideal location (I wasn't that excited about people seeing a printer or homeschool art spread all over the floor as soon as they walked into our house), but it was what worked for our family. And guess what? We still rarely homeschool in that designated space. My daughter likes to work all over the house. Sometimes I find her on her bed or sitting at the kitchen table or on the couch snuggling with the pups while she learns. Sometimes, when the weather is nice, she goes out onto our covered back porch, taking all her study stuff with her. Sometimes, when she wants a more quiet study space, she goes into her little closet under the stairs that we've transformed into a hideout and I find her reading in there. Very rarely does she sit at her desk in the "designated homeschool space" and work.

So, why am I telling you all of this about our space? We have the homeschool space and we don't utilize it as we should because we homeschool just fine at our kitchen table and anywhere else in the house. So, you don't need to stress about where you will homeschool in your home. There are many ways to add a homeschool "space" or homeschool storage, no matter how big or small your place is. If you are lacking on space, you might consider a bunk or loft bed in the child's bedroom so that a desk and bookshelves can be placed under the raised bed. Or, you can even convert a regular closet (not even a walk-in, just a regular coat closet) to homeschool storage with shelves and a fold down desk that you can close up when the area is not in use. Don't forget that you will probably spend some of your homeschool time outside of the home at different classes and meet-ups. And, the library is still a great space to work!

So, don't stress out about a designated homeschooling space. Instead, concentrate more on where you will put your homeschool stuff and less on where your homeschooler will do their work. The former will help you stay organized and less stressed and the latter will just work itself out on its own.

Homeschool Homework 20

Assess your home and think about what you would like a homeschool space to look like. Do you want an entire classroom? Do you have space for a classroom? Do you want the learning space to be in the children's bedroom? Do you just need a closet space or some good bookshelves in the family room to organize books and supplies? Write down your thoughts about a homeschool classroom in your notebook or journal.

If you need more inspiration for creating or updating a homeschool space, check out these two posts on HomeschoolSuperFreak.com:

35 HOMESCHOOL ROOM IDEAS FOR SMALL SPACES

http://homeschoolsuperfreak.com/homeschool-room-ideas-for-small-spaces/

HOW TO PUT A SMALL HOMESCHOOL ROOM IN A BEDROOM

http://homeschoolsuperfreak.com/how-to-put-a-small-homeschool-room-in-a-bedroom/

Myth #21: "You'll never be able to have a sick day."

This is another one of those perplexing statements that homeschooling parents hear. I never know if people mean *I* won't be able to take a sick day myself or *my kid* won't be able to take a sick day? Either way . . .

Sick days for homeschool families are like sick days for everyone else. If your kid is sick, you stay home from "work" (in this case, homeschooling) and focus on getting your child better. It's the same when the parent is sick. When I'm sick, my daughter is now old enough to have independent study for that day. When she was younger, if I had a sick day we would have low-key learning or unschooling on that day, like lying in bed watching educational shows or reading or making art. Also, you can just take a day off.

Additionally, many homeschooling families do have support systems, so it's not unusual for a homeschool parent to call in reinforcements (parents, in-laws, family, homeschooling friends) when they need it. This is yet another reason why it's very important for you to build up a homeschool support system!

Related Myth: "You'll never be able to

take a vacation or a day off!"

For some reason, people think that homeschooling families will have less time to do things when they homeschool, but it is quite the opposite. Homeschooling is extremely flexible, which is one of the major benefits of doing it. We use travel as part of our learning process. The flexibility of homeschooling allows us to travel wherever we want, whenever we want, and there is always a great museum, park, or hands-on learning opportunity that we take advantage of while traveling. Not only does travel allow our homeschooler to learn about different cultures (even when traveling within the United States), but it also provides important life skills. By the age of four, my daughter knew how to pack her suitcase and navigate her way through airports and hotels, important skills that she will carry with her throughout her life.

Now, about that day off thing . . .

Here's a little secret: sometimes homeschoolers take a day off . . . even during the middle of a school week. *(Gasp!)* There are some weeks when we've had a particularly grueling schedule that I'll wake up and say to my daughter, "Today is a free learning day!" She needs a break from what has been going on and I need a break for some peace of mind. On those days, she gets to pick what she wants to do. Some days, she reads. Sometimes she gets out a canvas and paints about something that inspired her. Sometimes she builds a fantasy nature land in the backyard. Some of that time she might play games on her tablet, get out her Lego bricks, and yes, even watch television. Does this put us behind on studies? Nope. Honestly, it probably helps us because once we've had a break and our minds and bodies are more relaxed, we can clearly move onto the next task with more energy and commitment.

Remember, you control your homeschool schedule. (Yes, repeat it again! And again! And again!) If part of that is learning by travel, so be it (and yay for your family)! If that means an occasional day off to save some sanity and also enjoy the benefits of free play, then that's OK, too.

Homeschooling Homework 21

Take a break! Take some time to look back through the things you've journaled or written in your notebook so far. Use this time to reflect or write about some of the things you've been thinking about for homeschooling.

JACQUELINE WILSON

Myth #22: "Homeschool kids rely too much on their parents, so they'll never be independent."

If someone doesn't understand the process of homeschooling, they might (wrongly) assume that homeschooling parents dictate every moment of a child's day. However, many homeschool parents allow their kids to direct their own learning or a portion of their learning, which helps to create a level of autonomy and independence. For example, at our house we have certain subjects that are directed and others that my daughter takes charge of for herself. Then, on Fridays, we often have a free learning day where I ask her what she would like to learn about, or if there is a specific project she wants to work on, or if there is a field trip she wants to take. This choice and autonomy sets the stage for her to be independent and allows her to practice making her own choices in the future.

As we discussed earlier, many homeschooling families focus not only on academic learning, but also heavily on life skills. We give our kids regular chores and responsibilities. Homeschoolers may be tasked with taking care of siblings, or pets, or farm animals. They do the dishes and mow lawns. In most homeschooling families, there is an expectation that the kids contribute to helping out the family and helping around the house. Homeschoolers do all of this within the responsibilities of their homeschooling day. These are important ways that children build autonomy and are able to learn skills that carry over into adulthood.

Julie Lythcott-Haims, former Dean of Freshmen and Undergraduate Advising at Stanford University, told the *Boston Globe*, "When young people have been expected to roll up their sleeves and pitch in, and to ask how they can contribute to the household, it leads to a mind-set of pitching in in other settings, such as the workplace. [Not giving kids chores] deprives them of the satisfaction of applying their effort to a task and accomplishing it." Lynthcott-Haims goes on to say that you shouldn't worry about giving kids too many chores in conjunction with their school work, stating that juggling life and work helps prepare our children for a realistic future where they will be required to regularly multitask.

A University of Minnesota study also found that one of the best predictors of success in young adults was to start chores early on in their childhood. I always try to keep in mind, *"What kind of successful life is my child going to have if she excels at academia but can't even cook her own food or do her own laundry?"*

Homeschool Homework 22

Do you need to work on giving your children more independence in your family? Give some thought on how you can further foster independence and autonomy in your child. Does he or she need more chores? Can you allow your child to pick out his or her own outfits each day? Will allowing them more autonomy in their studies be helpful? Jot down your ideas about fostering independence in your journal or notebook.

JACQUELINE WILSON

Myth #23: "Homeschooling is too boring for kids."

Do you have a concern that learning at home will become too boring for your kids? Well, don't. **Remember, you control what and how your children learn at home.** You can make homeschooling as exciting (or, I guess, as boring) as you want. In all of our years of homeschooling, I've only heard my daughter say that she was bored a handful of times—and that was when we weren't doing school work! (I'll tell you why this might actually be a problem later.)

A great thing about homeschooling is that you can allow your children to direct some (or even all) of their learning. Your children can pick the topics that they're interested in and you can build lessons around those topics. This process can help combat boredom and keep your children engaged in their studies.

Remember that room in the movie *Willy Wonka & the Chocolate Factory* where Wonka finally opens the door to the Chocolate Room and all of the families *ooh* and *ahh*? Then they run in different directions to sample the candy and treats growing and flowing everywhere? That's how I feel about homeschooling! There are so many choices, things to learn, and ways to learn them that there is little time for monotony to set in. Sure, you may have certain times that you may have to follow a specific curriculum, but there is so much additional time for a rainbow of opportunities if you allow it!

Lastly—and we touched on this earlier—there are ample occasions for you to supplement your at-home learning with outside-the-home learning. So, while it may seem that learning at home each day is boring, it's actually the exact opposite because each day is usually very different than the day before.

And, About That Boredom Thing . . .

Now that we've talked about how homeschooling really isn't as boring as people think, let's talk about the benefits of boredom. That's right, **I said the benefits of boredom**.

Did you know that there are benefits to allowing your child to be bored on occasion? In today's fast paced society, we have conditioned ourselves to believe that we have to fill each moment of our child's schedule in order for them to have a contented and accomplished life. However, in a BBC.com interview, Dr. Teresa Belton cautioned us against being uneasy over not keeping our kids constantly busy. Dr. Belton acknowledges that "[society has] developed an expectation of being constantly occupied and constantly stimulated." She goes on to say that this mindset isn't necessarily a good thing.

According to *Psychology Today*, "Children who experience a lack of programmed activity are given an opportunity to demonstrate creativity, problem solving, and to develop motivational skills that may help them later in life." So, don't stress or feel guilt when your homeschoolers say, "I'm bored!" Instead, allow them the room (and lack of guidance) to be without direction, or to create their own craft, or to find ways to occupy their own time and just *be*.

One thing I did when my daughter was younger was to create busy bags. I would use brown paper lunch bags and go around the house and place random items into the bag. I didn't even give it thought—two pipe cleaners, a plastic spoon, some ribbon, a bottle of glitter, a marble, a gluestick, and some scrap paper—and then I would staple the top shut. I would spend some time and make an entire basket of busy bags like this. Then, when my daughter was "bored," she would pick a busy bag, open it up, and have to figure out something to do with the odd items. Sometimes she would make an art project. Other times she would make a game or an invention that she would use with one of her lessons. To be honest, I was always completely surprised and impressed with what she would make using just a few unrelated, random items.

Homeschool Homework 23

Give some thought to your schedule. How full is it? Are you always running to this class or that event? Are you guilty of the belief that your child must be in every event or activity in order to have an enriched, successful life? Have you built in any time for your kids to just *be bored*? Write your thoughts and ideas about your busy schedule in your journal or notebook.

Homeschool Homework Extras

If you would like further reading on boredom, check out the following post on HomeschoolSuperFreak.com:

THIS ONE UNUSUAL CHANGE COULD MAKE YOUR HOMESCHOOLER MORE SUCCESSFUL

http://homeschoolsuperfreak.com/boredom-is-good-for-the-brain/

If you want to make some busy bags but need inspiration, check out the following post on HomeschoolSuperFreak.com:

BUSY BAGS FOR BUSTING BOREDOM

http://homeschoolsuperfreak.com/busy-bags-for-busting-boredom-summer-crafts-homeschool-parenting/

Myth #24: "Your kids will never be able to distinguish between your parent role and your teacher role."

The first time I heard this (but not the last time) was from my husband when I initially told him that I wanted to homeschool. "How will she take you seriously as a teacher and not just think of you as 'mom?'" he asked.

At that point, I didn't have an answer for him. He and I were both traditionally schooled and we were so immersed in the traditional way of education that the most important thing didn't even occur to us: it doesn't matter if my child sees me as a mom *and* a teacher. That fact has absolutely no bearing on how my child (and your child) can and will learn. I am an authority figure that is respected in my child's life, no matter if I'm being a mom or if I'm being a teacher. I'm the same person as "mom" as I am as "teacher." I don't magically change from fun happy mom to strict teacher when we walk into our homeschool classroom. I'm the same person in both roles.

The question about the need to distinguish between the parent role versus the teacher role brings up an even bigger issue: how we are conditioned to learn based on our past experiences.

Deschooling

Deschooling is a term that is used to describe a decompression period that a child should be allowed when switching from traditional school to another method of education, like homeschooling. For example, if a child has attended traditional school, he or she has been conditioned to raise a hand to speak, ask permission to go to the bathroom, sit at a desk quietly for several hours on end, and eat lunch (or do other things) on a specific schedule. This is very different from homeschooling. Getting out of those traditional habits and disconnecting from the traditional way of schooling doesn't just happen on the first day of homeschooling. Jeanne Faulconer, author of TheHomeschoolMom.com, states, "Parents who are new to homeschooling and have taken a child out of school should expect the first days, weeks, and months of homeschooling to be hugely affected by the process of deschooling."

Think about it this way: have you ever had a job or a responsibility where you had to get up early each day—maybe at 5 or 6 a.m.? What happens when you go on vacation and you have a chance to sleep later? Chances are, your body clock still wakes you up at five in the morning. It may take a few days (or even a week) for you to decompress and get out of your schedule before your body lets you sleep in a little later. The same thing happens with school. Your child needs time to decompress and allow the body and mind time to readjust to a different way of doing things. And, you need that time to change your way of thinking, too!

Deschooling versus Unschooling

Remember, **unschooling** is a philosophy of learning outside of the norm that often allows the child to choose how and what he or she wants to learn; while **deschooling** is the process of decompressing from the traditional methods of education. During deschooling, you might let your child sleep in, choose his or her own books to read, and direct if they want to go to the zoo, a nature hike, or the museum that day. Or, maybe your child wants to watch some videos on learning how to draw cartoons. Or, maybe during your deschooling time you travel to different areas and experience different cultures.

During the deschooling process, you may actually use the philosophy of unschooling. For example, maybe your child expressed an interest in learning more about birds in your state. During deschooling, your child may naturally gravitate toward library books about birds, or ask to see the traveling Audubon exhibit that he saw on a commercial, or maybe your child wants to go on a bird watching nature hike. Jan Hunt, of NaturalChild.org, writes, "Unschooling children, free from the intimidation of public embarrassment and failing marks, retain their openness to new exploration," which is something that many of us lose during traditional schooling.

These facets of the unschooling philosophy are helpful during the deschooling process of switching from traditional thinking to a more open educational concept like homeschooling. However, after deschooling you may decide to choose another homeschool methodology that is not unschooling. After deschooling, you may decide that you want to follow the Charlotte Mason method or an eclectic method. Or, you may decide that unschooling is a good fit for your family.

There is no set time for deschooling. For some homeschoolers, they may deschool for a week or two before moving on to scheduled activities. Other homeschoolers may find that up to three months is necessary for deschooling and becoming accustomed to learning at home. It's up to you to determine what works best for your family because every family is different. Plus, there are no wrong answers!

Why You Might Want To Consider Deschooling, No Matter Where You Are In Your Stage of Homeschooling

So, when should you deschool? You should strongly consider deschooling if you are moving your children from traditional school to homeschool. If you have been traditionally schooled then it is beneficial for you to get into the correct mindset of homeschooling, too. Even if you haven't been in school for years, it is still all you know. Decompressing from that style of learning will help you be a better homeschooling parent. You will need to go through some level of decompressing and "unlearning" before you can move into homeschooling.

Remember, children are natural learners, so you don't need to worry about them "falling behind" during the deschooling period. John Holt, author of *How Children Learn*, states, "If left alone, children will know instinctively what method is best for them. Caring and observant parents soon learn that it is safe and appropriate to trust this knowledge . . . Perceptive parents are aware that there are many different ways to learn something, and they trust their children to know which ways are best for them."

Homeschool Homework 24

Reflect on your methods and beliefs about education. Do you need to spend some time deschooling, both for yourself and your child? Write down any notes or thoughts you have about deschooling in your journal or notebook.

JACQUELINE WILSON

Myth #25: "You have to listen to what the public school system tells you, so you're better off just sending your kids to regular school."

The response to this myth varies based on where you live. In some states, homeschooling families are required to follow state curricula (or the equivalent), while in other states parents have a great deal more freedom and independence and can choose the curricula they teach their children. According to ProPublica.org, 33 states require certain subjects to be taught, but not all of those states have an assessment to determine if the subjects were taught. The other states allow homeschoolers to teach the subjects and curricula using the method or philosophy that best fits their family.

In the states that require specific curricula, parents are generally still able to teach the curricula how they want and when they want, making their own schedules. Additionally, homeschooling families in those states are allowed to supplement their learning with other curricula and learning tools. Even in the most stringent homeschooling states, parents still have the ability to tailor and control a portion of the learning.

It is also important to discuss the filing of a notice to

homeschool if you are switching from a traditional school to a home school. In some states, the parent must file a notice with the school district notifying them of their intent to homeschool. Other states have more relaxed homeschooling laws and letters of intent may not be required. These states may also allow parents complete control of their child's academic life with little to no oversight or reporting. This is one of the many reasons why it's so important to understand the homeschooling laws that are specific to your state because they vary greatly.

If you are new to homeschooling, or even if you've been homeschooling previously, you need to be aware of the requirements for the state where you reside and stay up on any changes. One of the best ways to do this is to find a Facebook homeschool group that covers homeschool laws and issues specific to your state. In my state, we have a really great organization that stays on top of all the laws, requirements, and political issues that could affect homeschoolers. On more than one occasion, I've been made aware of homeschool requirements for my state that I previously didn't know about. (Another reason to be active on social media!)

Homeschool Homework 25

Visit the following link and click on *State Mandated Subjects*:

https://projects.propublica.org/graphics/homeschool

Is your state one that is listed as mandating specific subjects?

Next, search the internet for "state mandated homeschool curriculum [your state]." Research what the curriculum requirements are for your state. If you're new to homeschooling, note the requirements in your journal or notebook. If you've been homeschooling for some time, are you meeting your state requirements?

Lastly, search Facebook to see if there is a homeschool group in your state that covers state homeschooling requirements. If you find one, join the group so you can stay updated!

JACQUELINE WILSON

Myth #26: "Your kids will never go to prom."

We had to break up the seriousness of some of the recent topics with a myth that is easily in the top 10 comments that homeschooling parents hear: "But what about prom?"

For real, people say this to homeschooling families.

As I've mentioned, I went to traditional school. During that time, I attended three high school proms . . . and they were fun. I enjoyed finding beautiful dresses, getting dressed up, and dancing. However, I can say that the topic of missing prom never crossed my mind when I decided to homeschool my daughter. I think that's why it always surprises me when it's at the top of the list of things people say to homeschooling families.

I've wondered why people ask about prom and why is it a top question? I think (and I can only guess here) that it goes back to people thinking homeschooled kids get no opportunities for socialization. *(See: Myth #3)* However, I am surprised that a school dance is on the top of society's mind when talking about things they think kids will miss out on when homeschooling.

If missing prom is one of your homeschooling

concerns, then I'm going to make your day: homeschoolers actually do have proms! (Really!) During prom season when parents of traditionally schooled kids are posting pictures online of their kids dressed up and posing for prom, I see the same pictures from some homeschooling parents! Homeschoolers really do get out of their pajamas and get dressed up (sometimes)! And, some of us even listen to music and—wait for it—*dance*! (Insert collective *Footloose gasp*.)

Since homeschooling is becoming more mainstream, there are now many groups and organizations that hold proms for homeschooling families. It's the same experience that kids get in traditional school—homeschoolers dress up, they rent cars, they go with groups of their friends, they eat at special restaurants, they pose for pictures, and they have a great time. So, if this is one of your worries about homeschooling, don't let it be. There are opportunities for homeschoolers to go to prom!

Homeschool Homework 26

Search the internet for "Homeschool Proms" and check out some of the listings for the topic. If you're interested in this topic, search "homeschool proms" on Facebook to see if groups exist for your area and to see homeschool prom pictures. Or, search the internet for homeschool proms in your state and, in your notebook or journal, write down the groups and organizations that provide them for your state.

JACQUELINE WILSON

Myth #27: "Go ahead, homeschool your kid, but you won't have any support."

It's true, you do have to build your own support network when you homeschool. There is no parent-teacher organization that helps you meet other parents at school. There are no required school activities where you see the same parents over and over and over and . . . well, you get the point. And, I'm going to rip off this Band-Aid right now, there will be unsupportive friends and family members who, at times (especially in the beginning), will make you feel completely alone. But there is good news: you're not alone at all and you can have a support system!

Remember, the most recent statistics estimate that there are over 1.7 million homeschoolers. I happen to think the number is probably higher since many homeschooling parents may not participate in public educational surveys. Although, you do have to work to create your own group of homeschooling families for support (and fun!), there are many opportunities to do this.

Remember when I told you that businesses and organizations are now starting to take notice of homeschooling families and add homeschool classes and activities because they don't want to miss out on a revenue opportunity? This is good news for you because it means more homeschool classes and meet-ups where you get introduced to other homeschooling families and can start to form your own homeschool "tribe." I've watched our local library over the last year morph from offering a homeschool meet-up or class occasionally, to offering full schedules of classes on a regular basis. It's an exciting time for homeschooling with many opportunities to build your own support group!

An Important Reminder: Build An Online Support Network

A really cool facet to homeschooling at this point in time (as opposed to even just a few years ago), is that the online homeschooling presence is huge right now. There are websites, blogs, Facebook groups, Instagram accounts, Snapchats, Twitter feeds, and so much more! Even if you live in a remote area where your physical homeschooling network is pretty much nonexistent, you can still create an amazing, online group of homeschool supporters.

When I look at homeschool statistics on Facebook for business purposes, they show some homeschool audiences being well over 2 million people—that's 2 million people that you have the opportunity to connect with on just one platform! I regularly use my online homeschool connections to ask for input on areas where I may be stuck, to get recommendations for curricula, and just for laughs and support on days when I'm feeling overwhelmed. It really does help!

Homeschool Homework 27

Search the internet for "homeschool meetups [your city, state]." If there are no results, widen your search for just your state. Now, repeat the process on Facebook. Are there groups that look interesting to you? Write down in your journal or notebook one or two groups that you want to try out, and then join the online group or try a new meet up!

Write down a goal for meet ups. Maybe you'll shoot for joining one new Facebook group or meet up with one new homeschooling group each month? Remember, being exposed to new groups is how you grow your homeschooling network and support group, a must-have for a homeschooling family.

JACQUELINE WILSON

Myth #28: "You can't homeschool because your child has special needs / is struggling / learns differently."

Having a child who needs special, one-on-one attention (for whatever reason) makes them a great candidate for homeschooling. Additionally, if a child has special needs that require regular appointments or medical visits throughout the week, it is difficult to schedule those around a public school day. That's where the flexibility of a homeschool schedule comes in handy!

The Homeschool Legal Defense Association (HSLDA) lists the following reasons homeschooling may be helpful when dealing with special needs:

*For **learning disabled children** who function best with 'real-life problems' rather than artificial worksheet tasks, homeschooling may be ideal.*

*For **medically sensitive children**, learning at home provides the opportunity for careful monitoring.*

*For **attention deficit children** who function best with uniquely structured time and fewer distractions, homeschooling usually proves to be the answer.*

Some parents are choosing to transition their

children with special needs into homeschool so that they can tailor learning, meet the specific needs of their child, and provide extra support, all while knowing that they are in a safe and secure environment without judgment. Just like with any reason to homeschool, parents do not need specialized training or certification to homeschool their children with any type of specialized needs.

But What About Resources and Support?

One fear of parents new to homeschooling is that they may not be able to find the same special needs resources or support sometimes provided by the public school system. While families always have the opportunity to seek private resources, there may also be some public school resources available to homeschool families who have children with specialized needs. According to the HSLDA, "About 90% of funding for public school special education programs come from the state—not the federal government." They go on to say, "The states can distribute their 90% in any way they choose. Some states have enacted laws that provide services to 'homeschool' students . . ."

Another way homeschooling families can find support is by searching for special needs homeschooling groups, both locally and online. These groups can provide insight and advice into moving forward and covering specialized needs while homeschooling.

Homeschool Homework 28

Do you fall into the category discussed in this chapter? If so, visit the link below and see if there are public school resources available for your homeschooled child. (Also, be sure to read the HSLDA information on the cons of using public school resources for your homeschooler.) Visit:

https://www.hslda.org/strugglinglearner/sn_states.asp

Then, search Facebook for "special needs homeschooling." You will find pages and groups that you can join for support, advice, and answers!

JACQUELINE WILSON

Myth #29: "Your kid will miss out on *so much* not going to regular school."

"Oh really? Like what?"

That's my real response when someone makes that statement to me. I'm naturally curious what they think my daughter will be missing out on by not going to a traditional school. Most often, people can't answer right away. Or, they say things like "prom," "sports," "friends," or something similar. Again, most of those types of answers come from people not fully understanding homeschooling.

But, what else will homeschooled kids miss out on? Will they miss out on sitting still in a classroom for hours on end? Will they miss out on interacting with a diverse group of people of all ages and backgrounds because they're not in one classroom with the same age group? Will they miss out on regular hands-on learning inside and outside? Will they miss out on getting up very early to ride a bus and then spending hours on homework each evening when they come home? Will my homeschooled kid miss out on the peer pressure to dress, think, speak, and act a certain way? And, what about bullying? Clearly, I could go on and on. (Not to say that there aren't many positive sides to traditional schooling, because clearly there are.)

A homeschooling journey is what a family makes it. That means if you have homeschooled kids who want to be extremely active in outside activities, then that's what your child will be exposed to. It's no different than a traditionally schooled kid. There are traditionally schooled kids who are super involved and experience everything, and there are quiet or reserved kids who are more comfortable with one or two close friends and focusing on one (or no) extracurricular activities. It's the same for homeschooled kids. There are plenty of life and learning experiences to go around for everyone, no matter where they school. So no, I don't think my homeschooled child is going to miss out on "so much" by not going to traditional school.

Homeschool Homework 29

If you're new to homeschooling are there things you're worried that your kids will miss out on by not going to traditional school? List those in your notebook or journal. Then, brainstorm alternative ways you can help provide those types of experiences during homeschooling.

Myth #30: "Homeschooling just isn't a 'proper education.'"

If you've made it to the end of this book, you probably already know that homeschooling is as "proper" as traditional education. No, homeschooling is not illegal. No, you are not going to jail just for homeschooling your child. Yes, your homeschooled child can get socialization and they will make friends and develop relationships. Your homeschooled child may even be able to play public school sports and go to prom! And, your homeschooler can even go to college (if that is a path he or she chooses). As the homeschooling movement continues to grow, the opportunities will only continue to increase.

The End Is Just The Beginning!

If you're new to homeschooling, or you're just changing up some of your homeschooling processes, you may be feeling uncomfortable right now. That's OK! Ending things pushes us out of our comfort zone, but the end of one thing is the beginning of something else! And, if your new beginning involves homeschooling, then you're in for a fun ride!

Homeschool Homework 30

Congratulations! You made it to the last homeschool homework assignment!

Take some time to look back through your journal or notebook. Follow up on the items where you had questions. Also, spend some time journaling about homeschooling now that you've made it through the book.

Other Silly Things Homeschoolers Hear

There are many other myths, misconceptions, and pieces of misinformation that homeschooling families hear, but some of them didn't warrant an entire section in this book. That doesn't mean you can't chuckle along with some of the more, um, *unusual* things that homeschooling families hear. (These are real questions and statements said regularly to homeschooling families.)

Lucky you! You just get to play all day!

My daughter hears this one at least a couple of times each month, usually when we are out in public during "regular" school hours. The conversation goes something like this:

Person: "Oh, is school out today?"

My daughter: "No, I homeschool."

Person: "Lucky you! That means you just get to play all day!"

OK, then.

How will your child know how to stand in lines?

Apparently, society spends a great deal of time

thinking about standing in lines, because this is a **common** question that homeschooling families hear. So, how do our homeschooled kids know how to stand in lines? It's called common sense. It's not rocket science. We don't need school for that.

How will your homeschooled kid date?

Probably much the same way that all of us dated: we meet someone we're interested in and we go out with that person. Homeschooled kids are *(gasp)* allowed to talk to and interact with other kids. At some point, they may even want to date one of those other kids. So easy, right?

How will your homeschooled child learn to drive?

Again, probably the same way that most of us did: we signed up for a driver's education course. They give those publicly all around the country.

Do you live on a farm (have electricity, get to watch television, etc.)?

No, but I do love goats. (Does that count?) Some homeschooling families do live on farms. (The same way some traditionally schooled families do.) A few live "off the grid" where they are self-sufficient and don't rely on public utilities. (The same way a few traditionally schooled families do.) Some homeschooled kids aren't allowed to watch television or have electronic games or tablets. (The same way some traditionally schooled children aren't allowed those things.) However, the majority of us are just like traditionally schooled families, we just go to school at home.

Don't you want your child to be normal?

Can you define normal? I mean, I run a website called "Homeschool Super Freak" so I'm guessing that my "normal" might be a little different than most people's "normal." Besides, I find "normal" overrated, don't you?

JACQUELINE WILSON

THANK YOU!

Thank you for purchasing *It's Homeschooling, Not Solitary Confinement*!

If you enjoyed the book,
we would love your 5 star review on Amazon.com
to help us reach other homeschoolers!

We're excited to join you on your homeschooling journey!
Let's connect at online at:

Facebook.com/HomeschoolSuperFreak
Instagram.com/HomeschoolSuperFreak
Twitter.com/HSSuperFreak

Visit us at:

HomeschoolSuperFreak.com

References

MYTH 1

"Home Schooling - History, Legal Background, Legal Trends, Effects, Future Implications". Education.stateuniversity.com. N.p., 2017. Web. 27 June 2016.

<http://education.stateuniversity.com/pages/2050/Home-Schooling.html>.

MYTH 2

"Education And Homeschooling: State Laws - Findlaw". Findlaw. Web. 7 July 2016.

<http://education.findlaw.com/education-options/education-and-homeschooling-state-laws.html>.

"Home Schooling - History, Legal Background, Legal Trends, Effects, Future Implications". Education.stateuniversity.com. Web. 13 Oct. 2016.

<http://education.stateuniversity.com/pages/2050/Home-Schooling.html>.

"Homeschool Laws In Your State". HSLDA. Web. 27 June 2016.

<https://www.hslda.org/laws/>.

"Massachusetts Homeschool State Laws". Home School Facts. Web. 13 Oct. 2016.

<http://www.homeschoolfacts.com/state-

laws/massachusetts-homeschool-state-laws.html>.

Patterson, Mary Jo, and Ruth Martin. "GHEA - Article Library - History Of Homeschooling In The US And GA". Ghea.org. N.p., 2009. Web. 9 Sept. 2016.

<https://www.ghea.org/pages/articles/focus.php?ID=30&parent=45>.

Sommerville, Scott. "The Politics Of Survival: Home Schoolers And The Law". HSLDA.org. N.p., 2001. Web. 26 Aug. 2016.

MYTH 3

Michael F., Haverluck. "Socialization: Homeschooling Vs. Schools - US - CBN News - Christian News 24-7 - CBN.Com". Cbn.com. N.p., 2007. Web. 13 Oct. 2016.

<http://www.cbn.com/cbnnews/us/2007/may/socialization-homeschooling-vs-schools/>.

"The Definition Of Socialization". Dictionary.com. Web. 13 Oct. 2016.

<http://www.dictionary.com/browse/socialization?s=t>.

"The Definition Of Socialized". Dictionary.com. Web. 13 Oct. 2016.

<http://www.dictionary.com/browse/socialized?s=t>.

MYTH 4

"Reasons Parents Homeschool". Coalition for Responsible Home Education. Web. 14 Oct. 2016.

<http://www.responsiblehomeschooling.org/homeschooling-101/reasons-parents-homeschool/>.

"Statistics About Non-Public Education In The United States". Www2.ed.gov. Web. 14 Oct. 2016.

<https://www2.ed.gov/about/offices/list/oii/nonpublic/statistics.html>.

MYTH 5

"Parent Qualifications". Coalition for Responsible Home Education. Web. 1 Nov. 2016.

<https://www.responsiblehomeschooling.org/policy-issues/current-policy/parent-qualifications/>

MYTH 6

"Classical Education". Classicalconversations.com. Web. 11 Nov. 2016.

<https://www.classicalconversations.com/classical/classical-education>.

"What Is The Charlotte Mason Method? — Simply Charlotte Mason". *Simply Charlotte Mason*. Web. 3 June 2017.

<https://simplycharlottemason.com/what-is-the-charlotte-mason-method/>.

MYTH 10

Bentley, Vicki. "What Does It Cost To Homeschool?". www.hslda.org. N.p., 2013. Web. 11 Dec. 2016. <https://www.hslda.org/earlyyears/Costs.asp>

"Education Spending Per Student By State". Governing.com. Web. 11 Dec. 2016. <http://www.governing.com/gov-data/education-data/state-education-spending-per-pupil-data.html>

Lawrence, Julia. "Homeschooling Ranks Growing Nationwide". Education News. N.p., 2012. Web. 11 Dec. 2016. <http://www.educationnews.org/parenting/number-of-homeschoolers-growing-nationwide/>

Wood, Genevieve. "In One State, More Children Homeschool Than Attend Private Schools.". The Daily Signal. N.p., 2014. Web. 11 Dec. 2016. <http://dailysignal.com/2014/09/08/one-state-children-homeschool-attend-private-schools-shouldnt-shock/>

MYTH 11

"State Laws Concerning Participation of Homeschool Students in Public School Activities." State Laws Concerning Participation of Homeschool Students in Public School Activities (n.d.): n. pag. 21 Nov. 2016. Web. 15 Dec. 2016.

<https://www.hslda.org/docs/nche/Issues/E/Equal_Access.pdf>

"Tim Tebow Laws and Homeschool Athletes." Home School Facts. HomeschoolFacts.com, 21 May 2015. Web. 15 Dec. 2016. <http://www.homeschoolfacts.com/are-tim-tebow-laws-a-touchdown-for-homeschool-students/>

Myth 13

Anderson, Jenny. "From Finland, an Intriguing School-Reform Model." The New York Times. The New York Times, 12 Dec. 2011. Web. 20 Jan. 2017. <http://www.nytimes.com/2011/12/13/education/from-finland-an-intriguing-school-reform-model.html>.

Brown, Kalee. "Finland To Become The First Country In The World To Get Rid Of All School Subjects." Collective Evolution. Collective Evolution, 04 Apr. 2017. Web. 10 Apr. 2017. <http://www.collective-evolution.com/2017/04/04/finland-to-become-the-first-country-in-the-world-to-get-rid-of-all-school-subjects/>.

Day, Kelly. "11 Ways Finland's Education System Shows Us That "Less Is More"." Filling My Map. FillingMyMap.com, 12 May 2015. Web. 15 Jan. 2017. <https://fillingmymap.com/2015/04/15/11-ways-finlands-education-system-shows-us-that-less-is-more/>.

Edwards, Laurie. "Preschoolers Need Structure ... or Don't They?" Education.com. Education.com, 11 May 2009. Web. 20 Jan. 2017. <https://www.education.com/magazine/article/preschoolers-structure-or-not/>.

MYTH 14

Samburg, Bridget. "Our Kids Don't Belong in School." Boston Magazine. Boston Magazine, Sept. 2015. Web. 15 Feb. 2017. <http://www.bostonmagazine.com/news/article/2015/08/25/homeschooling-in-boston/>.

Schmidt, TJ. "Colleges: Are You a Real Homeschool Graduate?" HSLDA | Colleges: Are You a Real Homeschool Graduate? HSLDA, 24 Jan. 2017. Web. 10 Feb. 2017. <http://www.hslda.org/hs/state/fl/201701240.asp>.

Tate, Allison Slater. "Colleges Welcome Growing Number of Homeschooled Students."NBCNews.com. NBCUniversal News Group, 17 Feb. 2016. Web. 17 Feb. 2017. <http://www.nbcnews.com/feature/college-game-plan/colleges-welcome-growing-number-homeschooled-students-n520126>.

Weller, Chris. "There's a New Path to Harvard and It's Not in a Classroom." Business Insider. Business Insider, 03 Sept. 2015. Web. 16 Feb. 2017. <http://www.businessinsider.com/homeschooling-is-the-new-path-to-harvard-2015-9>.

MYTH 15

Becker, Hollee Actman. "Family Vacations Have Long-Lasting Impact on Kids' Happiness."Parents. Parents.com, 21 Feb. 2017. Web. 03 June 2017. <http://www.parents.com/health/parents-news-

now/family-vacations-have-long-lasting-impact-on-kids-happiness/>.

Weller, Chris. "There's a New Path to Harvard and It's Not in a Classroom." Business Insider. Business Insider, 03 Sept. 2015. Web. 03 May 2017. <http://www.businessinsider.com/homeschooling-is-the-new-path-to-harvard-2015-9>.

MYTH 16

"11 Facts about Literacy in America." DoSomething.org | Volunteer for Social Change. Do Something, n.d. Web. 23 Feb. 2017. <https://www.dosomething.org/us/facts/11-facts-about-literacy-america>.

Dougherty, Chrys, and Steve Fleming. "Getting Students on Track to College and Career Readiness: How Many Catch Up from Far Behind?" ACT.org. ACT, 2012. Web. 30 May 2017. <http://media.act.org/documents/ACT_RR2012-9.pdf+>.

"LITERACY FACTS & STATS." LITERACY FACTS & STATS (n.d.): n. pag. Reading Is Fundamental. Reading Is Fundamental. Web. 23 Feb. 2017. <http://www.rif.org/pdf/Literacy-Facts-Stats.pdf>.

Speer, Laura, and Florencia Gutierrez. "Kids Count Data Book." Annie E Casey Foundation. Annie E Casey Foundation, 2016. Web. 30 May 2017. <http://www.aecf.org/m/resourcedoc/aecf-the2016kidscountdatabook-2016.pdf+>.

Starr, Linda. "Student Report Cards: Do They Earn an A -- or a "Needs Improvement?""Education World: Student Report Cards: Do They Earn an A -- or a Needs Improv...Education World, 1998. Web. 23 Feb. 2017.
<http://www.educationworld.com/a_issues/issues035.shtml>.

MYTH 19

Redford, Jeremey, Danielle Battle, and Stacey Bielick. "Homeschooling in the United States: 2012." (n.d.): n. pag. National Center for Education Stastistics. Department of Education, Apr. 2017. Web. 26 May 2017.
<https://nces.ed.gov/pubs2016/2016096rev.pdf>.

MYTH 22

Albernaz, Ami. "Research Indicates Sparing the Chores, Spoils Children and Their Future Selves - The Boston Globe." BostonGlobe.com. Boston Globe, 08 Dec. 2015. Web. 27 May 2017.
<https://www.bostonglobe.com/lifestyle/2015/12/08/research-indicates-sparing-chores-spoils-children-and-their-future-selves/ZLvMznpC5btmHtNRXXhNFJ/story.html>.

INVOLVING CHILDREN IN HOUSEHOLD TASKS: IS IT WORTH THE EFFORT? (n.d.): n. pag. INVOLVING CHILDREN IN HOUSEHOLD TASKS: IS IT WORTH THE EFFORT? University of Minnesota, Sept. 2002. Web. 27 May 2017. <http://ghk.h-cdn.co/assets/cm/15/12/55071e0298a05_-_Involving-

children-in-household-tasks-U-of-M.pdf>.

MYTH 23

Richardson, Hannah. "Children Should Be Allowed to Get Bored, Expert Says." BBC News. BBC, 23 Mar. 2013. Web. 29 May 2017. <http://www.bbc.com/news/education-21895704>.

Ungar, Michael. "Let Kids Be Bored (Occasionally)." Psychology Today. Sussex Publishers, 24 June 2012. Web. 28 May 2017. <https://www.psychologytoday.com/blog/nurturing-resilience/201206/let-kids-be-bored-occasionally>.

MYTH 24

Faulconer, Jeanne. "From School to Homeschool: What Is Deschooling?" The Home School Mom. The Home School Mom, 04 Mar. 2014. Web. 29 May 2017. <https://www.thehomeschoolmom.com/school-homeschool-what-is-deschooling/>.

Hunt, Jan. "Nurturing Children's Natural Love of Learning." The Natural Child Project. The Natural Child Project, n.d. Web. 29 May 2017. <http://www.naturalchild.org/jan_hunt/unschooling.html>.

MYTH 25

Huseman, Jessica. "Homeschooling Regulations." Homeschooling Regulations by State. Pro Publica, 27 Aug. 2015. Web. 07 June 2017. <https://projects.propublica.org/graphics/homeschool>.

MYTH 28

"Special Education Provisions in the 50 States and Territories." HSLDA | Special Needs : Special Education Provisions in the 50 States and Territories. HSLDA, n.d. Web. 31 May 2017. <https://www.hslda.org/strugglinglearner/sn_states.asp>.

"Special Needs Child Thrives by Homeschooling, School District Doesn't Understand How." HSLDA | Special Needs : Introduction. HSLDA, n.d. Web. 31 May 2017. <https://www.hslda.org/strugglinglearner/>.

Made in the USA
Lexington, KY
04 November 2018